THE
13 STEPS TO
RICHES

BASED ON THE WORK BY NAPOLEON HILL IN

THINK AND GROW RICH

CREATED BY MULTI #1 INTERNATIONAL BESTSELLING AUTHOR & AWARD WINNING SPEAKER ON HABITS

ERIK "MR AWESOME" SWANSON

THE
13 STEPS TO
RICHES

Featuring
Erik Swanson & Loral Langemeier

TRANSMUTATION
VOLUME 10

HABITUDE
WARRIOR

Foreword by Lexi Vernsey

TESTIMONIALS
THE 13 STEPS TO RICHES

"What an honor to collaborate with so many personal development leaders from around the world as we Co-Author together honoring the amazing principles by Napoleon Hill in this new book series, *The 13 Steps to Riches*, by Habitude Warrior and Erik "Mr. Awesome" Swanson. Well done, "Mr. Awesome," for putting together such an amazing series. If you want to up-level your life, read every book in this series and learn to apply each of these time-tested steps and principles."

Denis Waitley ~ Author of *Psychology of Winning & The NEW Psychology of Winning—Top Qualities of a 21st Century Winner*

"Just as *Think and Grow Rich* reveals the 13 steps to success discovered by Napoleon Hill after interviewing the richest people around the world (and many who considered themselves failures) in the early 1900s, *The 13 Steps to Riche*s, produced by Habitude Warrior and Erik Swanson takes a modern look at those same 13 steps. It brings together many of today's personal development leaders to share their stories of how *The 13 Steps to Riches* have created and propelled their own successes. I am honored to participate and share the power of Faith in my life. If you truly want to accelerate reaching the success you deserve, read every volume of *The 13 Steps to Riches*."

Sharon Lechter ~ 5 Time N.Y. Times Bestselling Author. Author of *Think and Grow Rich for Women*, Co-Author of *Exit Rich, Rich Dad Poor Dad, Three Feet from Gold, Outwitting the Devil* and *Success and Something Greater*

"The most successful book on personal achievement ever written is now being elaborated upon by many of the world's top thought leaders. I'm honored to Co-Author this series on the amazing principles from Napoleon Hill, in *The 13 Steps to Riches*, by Habitude Warrior, Erik "Mr. Awesome" Swanson."

> *Jim Cathcart* ~ Bestselling Author of *Relationship Selling* and *The Acorn Principle*, among many others. Certified Speaking Professional (CSP) and Former President of the National Speakers Association (NSA)

"Some books are written to be read and placed on the shelf. Others are written to transform the reader, as they travel down a path of true transcendence and enlightenment. *The 13 Steps to Riches* by Habitude Warrior and Erik Swanson is the latter. Profoundly insightful, it revitalizes the techniques and strategies written by Napoleon Hill by applying a modern perspective, and a fearsome collaboration of some of the greatest minds and thought leaders from around the globe. A must-read for all of those who seek to break free of their current levels of success, and truly extract the greatness that lies within. It is an honor and a privilege to have been selected to participate, in what is destined to be the next historic chapter in the meteoric rise of many men and women around the world."

> *Glenn Lundy* ~ Husband to one, Father to 8, Automotive Industry Expert, Author of *The Morning 5*, Creator of the popular morning show "#riseandgrind," and the Founder of "Breakfast With Champions"

"How exciting to team up with the amazing Habitude Warrior community of leaders such as Erik Swanson, Sharon Lechter, John Assaraf, Denis Waitley and so many more transformational and self-help icons to bring you these timeless and proven concepts in the fields of success and wealth. *The 13 Steps to Riches* book series will help you reach your dreams and accomplish your goals faster than you have ever experienced before!"

Marie Diamond ~ Featured in *The Secret*, Modern-Day Spiritual Teacher, Inspirational Speaker, Feng Shui Master

"If you are looking to crystalize your mightiest dream, rekindle your passion, break through limiting beliefs and learn from those who have done exactly what you want to do - read this book! In this transformational masterpiece, *The 13 Steps to Riches*, self-development guru Erik Swanson has collected the sage wisdom and time-tested truths from subject matter experts and amalgamated it into a one-stop-shop resource library that will change your life forever!"

Dan Clark ~ Speaker Hall of Fame & N.Y. Times Bestselling Author of *The Art of Significance*

"Life has always been about who you surround yourself with. I am in excellent company with this collaboration from my fellow authors and friends, paying tribute to the life-changing principles by Napoleon Hill in this amazing new book series, *The 13 Steps to Riches*, organized by Habitude Warrior's founder and my dear friend, Erik Swanson. Hill said, 'Your big opportunity may be right where you are now.' This book series is a must-read for anyone who wants to change their lives and prosper, starting now."

Alec Stern ~ America's Startup Success Expert, Co-Founder of Constant Contact

"Finally a book series that encompasses the lessons the world needs to learn and apply, but in our modern day era. As I always teach my students to "Say YES, and then figure out how," I strongly urge you to do the same. Say YES to adding all of these 13 books in *The 13 Steps to Riches* book series into your success library and watch both your business as well as your personal life grow as a result."

Loral Langemeier ~ 5 Time N.Y. Times Bestselling Author, Featured in *The Secret*, Author of *The Millionaire Maker* and *YES! Energy - The Equation to Do Less, Make More*

"Napoleon Hill had a tremendous impact on my consciousness when I was very young – there were very few books nor the type of trainings that we see today to lead us to success. Whenever you have the opportunity to read and harness *The 13 Steps to Riches* as they are presented in this series, be happy (and thankful) that there were many of us out there applying the principles, testing the teachings, making the mistakes, and now being offered to you in a way that they are clear, simple and concise—with samples and distinctions that will make it easier for you to design a successful life which includes adding value to others, solving world problems, and making the world work for 100% of humanity... Read on... those dreams are about to come true!"

Doria Cordova ~ CEO of Money & You, Excellerated Business School, Global Business Developer, Ambassador of New Education

"Success leaves clues and the Co-Authors in this awesome book series, *The 13 Steps to Riches*, will continue the Napoleon Hill legacy with tools, tips and modern-day principals that greatly expand on the original masterpiece... *Think and Grow Rich*. If you are serious about living your life to the max, get this book series now!"

John Assaraf ~ Chairman & CEO NeuroGym, MrNeuroGym.com, N.Y. Times Bestselling Author of *Having It All, Innercise*, and *The Answer*. Also featured in *The Secret*

"Over the years, I have been blessed with many rare and amazing opportunities to invest my time and energy. These opportunities require a keen eye and immediate action. This is one of those amazing opportunities for you as a reader! I highly recommend you pick up every book in this series of *The 13 Steps to Riches* by Habitude Warrior and Erik Swanson! Learn from modern-day leaders who have embraced the lessons from the great Napoleon Hill in his classic book from 1937, *Think and Grow Rich*."

Kevin Harrington ~ Original "Shark" on Shark Tank, Creator of the Infomercial, Pioneer of the 'As Seen on TV' brand, Co-Author of *Mentor to Millions*

"When you begin your journey, you will quickly learn of the importance of the first step of *The 13 Steps To Riches*. A burning desire is the start of all worthwhile achievements. Erik 'Mr. Awesome' Swanson's newest book series contains a wealth of assistance to make your journey both successful and enjoyable. Start today... because tomorrow is not guaranteed on your calendar."

Don Green ~ 45 Years of Banking, Finance & Entrepreneurship, Bestselling Author of *Everything I Know About Success I Learned From Napoleon Hill* & *Napoleon Hill My Mentor: Timeless Principles to Take Your Success to the Next Level* & *Your Millionaire Mindset*

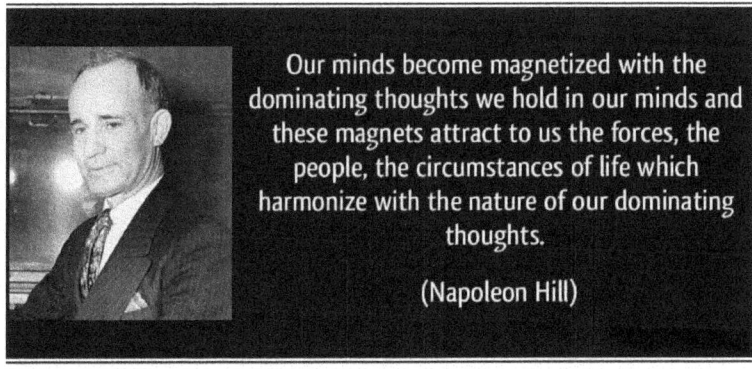

Our minds become magnetized with the dominating thoughts we hold in our minds and these magnets attract to us the forces, the people, the circumstances of life which harmonize with the nature of our dominating thoughts.

(Napoleon Hill)

Global Speakers Mastermind & Habitude Warrior Masterminds

Join us and become a member of our tribe! Our Global Speakers Mastermind is a virtual group of amazing thinkers and leaders who meet twice a month. Sessions are designed to be 'to the point' and focused while sharing fantastic techniques to grow your mindset as well as your pocketbooks. We also include famous guest speaker spots for our private Masterclasses. We also designate certain sessions for our members to mastermind with each other & and counsel on the topics discussed in our previous Masterclasses. It's time for you to join a tribe who truly cares about **YOU** and your future and start surrounding yourself with the famous leaders and mentors of our time. It is time for you to up-level your life, businesses, and relationships.

For more information to check out our Masterminds:
Team@HabitudeWarrior.com
www.DecideTobeAwesome.com

BECOME AN INTERNATIONAL
#1 BESTSELLING AUTHOR & SPEAKER

Habitude Warrior International has been highlighting award-winning Speakers and #1 Bestselling Authors for over 25 years. They know what it takes to become #1 in your field and how to get the best exposure around the world. If you have ever considered giving yourself the GIFT of becoming a well-known Speaker and a fantastically well known #1 Best-Selling Author, then you should email their team right away to find out more information in how you can become involved. They have the best of the best when it comes to resources in achieving the bestselling status in your particular field. Start surrounding yourself with the N.Y. Times Bestsellers of our time and start seeing your dreams become reality!

For more information to become a #1 Bestselling Author & Speaker on our Habitude Warrior Conferences Please text the word AUTHORS to 619-304-6268 And also go to:
www.DecideToBeAwesome.com

Napoleon Hill

I would like to personally acknowledge and thank the one and only Napoleon Hill for his work, dedication, and most importantly believing in himself. His unwavering belief in himself, whether he realized this or not, had been passed down from generation to generation to millions and millions of individuals across this planet including me!

I'm sure, at first, as many of us experience throughout our lives as well, he most likely had his doubts. Think about it. Being offered to work for Andrew Carnegie for a full 20 years with zero pay and no guarantee of success had to be a daunting decision. But, I thank you for making that decision years and years ago. It paved the path for countless many who have trusted in themselves and found success in their own rights. You gave us all hope, desire, and faith to bank on the most important energy in the world—ourselves!

For this, I thank you Sir, from the bottom of my heart and the top of all of our bank accounts. Let us all follow the 13 Steps to Riches and prosper in so many areas of our lives.

~ Erik "Mr. Awesome" Swanson
13 Time #1 Bestselling Author & Student of Napoleon Hill Philosophies

Lance Cpl. Dylan R. Merola, 20

It is our distinct honor to dedicate each one of *The 13 Steps to Riches* book volumes to each of the 13 United States Service Members who courageously lost their lives in Kabul in August 2021. Your honor, dignity, and strength will always be cherished and remembered.

~ Habitude Warrior Team

Lance Cpl. Dylan R. Merola, 20, of Rancho Cucamonga, California, a rifleman.

His awards and decorations include the National Defense Service Medal and Global War on Terrorism Service Medal. Additional awards pending approval may include Purple Heart, Combat Action Ribbon, and Sea Service Deployment Ribbon. We honor you and thank you for your ultimate sacrifice!

THE 13 STEPS TO RICHES
Featuring

DENIS WAITLEY ~ Author of *Psychology of Winning* & *The NEW Psychology of Winning—Top Qualities of a 21st Century Winner*, NASA's Performance Coach, Featured in *The Secret.* ~ www.DenisWaitley.com

SHARON LECHTER ~ 5 Time N.Y. Times Bestselling Author. Author of *Think and Grow Rich for Women*, Co-Author of *Exit Rich, Rich Dad Poor Dad, Three Feet from Gold, Outwitting the Devil* and *Success and Something Greater.* ~ www.SharonLechter.com

JIM CATHCART~ Bestselling Author of Relationship Selling and The Acorn Principle, among many others. Certified Speaking Professional (CSP) and Former President of the National Speakers Association (NSA). ~ www.Cathcart.com

MICHAEL E. GERBER ~ N.Y. Times Bestseller of the mega-bestselling theory for over two consecutive decades...*The E-Myth* Books. ~ www.MichaelEGerberCompanies.com

GLENN LUNDY ~ Husband to one, Father to 8, Automotive Industry Expert, Author of *The Morning 5*, Creator of the popular morning show "#riseandgrind," and the Founder of Breakfast With Champions. ~ www.GlennLundy.com

MARIE DIAMOND ~ Featured in *The Secret*, Modern Day Spiritual Teacher, Inspirational Speaker, Feng Shui Master.
~ www.MarieDiamond.com

DAN CLARK ~ Award Winning Speaker, Speaker Hall of Fame, N.Y. Times Bestselling Author of *The Art of Significance.*
~ www.DanClark.com

ALEC STERN ~ America's Startup Success Expert, Co-Founder of Constant Contact, Speaker, Mentor, and Investor.
~ www.AlecSpeaks.com

ERIK SWANSON ~ 13 Time #1 International Bestselling Author, Award-Winning Speaker, Featured on TEDx Talks and Amazon Prime TV. Founder & CEO of the Habitude Warrior Brand.
~ www.SpeakerErikSwanson.com

LORAL LANGEMEIER ~ 5 Time N.Y. Times Bestselling Author, Featured in *The Secret*, Author of *The Millionaire Maker* and *YES! Energy - The Equation to Do Less, Make More.*
~ www.LoralLangemeier.com

DORIA CORDOVA ~ CEO of Money & You, Excellerated Business School, Global Business Developer, Ambassador of New Education.
~ www.FridaysWithDoria.com

JOHN ASSARAF ~ Chairman & CEO NeuroGym, MrNeuroGym.com, New York Times Bestselling Author of *Having It All*, *Innercise*, and *The Answer*. Also featured in *The Secret*. ~ www.JohnAssaraf.com

 **KEVIN HARRINGTON** ~ Original "Shark" on the hit TV show Shark Tank, Creator of the Infomercial, Pioneer of the As Seen on TV brand, Co-Author of Mentor to Millions. ~ www.KevinHarrington.TV

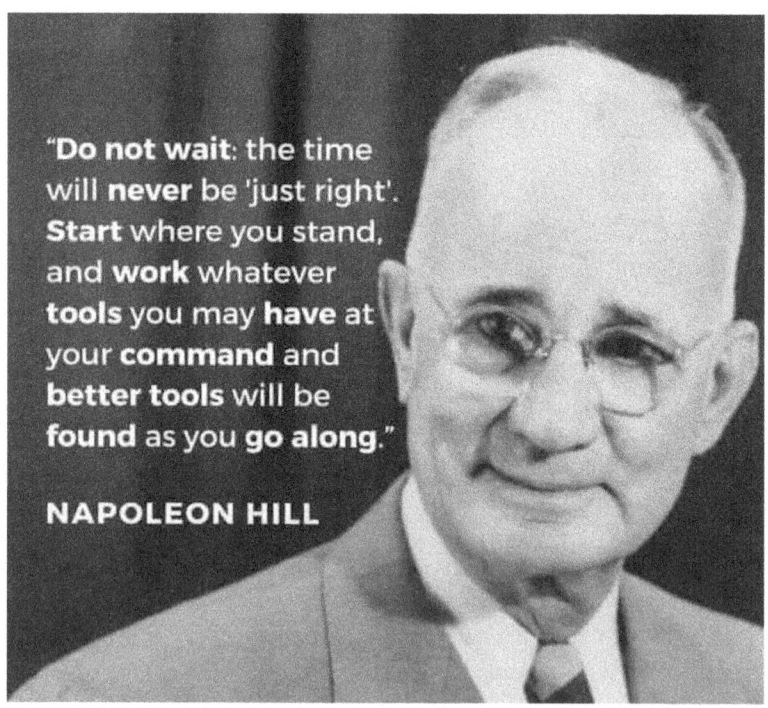

"**Do not wait**: the time will **never** be 'just right'. **Start** where you stand, and **work** whatever **tools** you may **have** at your **command** and **better tools** will be **found** as you **go along**."

NAPOLEON HILL

CONTENTS

ERIK SWANSON & DON GREEN

Once you give yourself the gift of reading Erik Swanson's newest book series, *The 13 Steps to Riches*, you are sure to realize why he has earned his nickname, "*Mr. Awesome*." Readers usually read books for two reasons – they want to be entertained or they want to improve their knowledge in a certain subject. Mr. Awesome's new book series will help you do both.

I urge you to not only read this great book series in it's entirety, but also apply the principles held within into your our life. Use the experience Erik Swanson has gained to reach your own level of success. I highly encourage you to invest in yourself by reading self-help materials, such as *The 13 Steps to Riches*, and I truly know you will discover that it will be one of the best investments you could ever make.

Don Green
Executive Director and CEO
The Napoleon Hill Foundation

FOREWORD
BY LEXI VERNSEY

"When any negative emotion presents itself in one's mind, it can be transmuted into a positive, or constructive emotion, by the simple procedure of changing one's thoughts. There is no other road to genius than through voluntary self-effort!"
~ Napoleon Hill

The Athlete

I was fifteen, going into the second semester of my freshman year. The school was not as bad as I thought, but I still had nerves. I decided I wanted to do track and field, thinking it would be a good way to get faster for soccer. Soccer had been my life forever and I was excited about the next soccer season. I knew I needed to get in better shape and faster. That's all I thought track would be. I never expected to have such an amazing experience.

I made some of my friends come to track with me. The first week was Hell Week and I'll tell you—it was hell. I had never run this much in my life. I was always good at running, but, that week, I was starting to question why. Then, one day, I heard the workout and decided I couldn't do it that day, so I decided to go practice with the jumpers because why not try something new and no running; I'm in!

We had to practice inside because there was still snow all over the track. I walked into practice and saw these big pads on the floor. I was nervous, but it was better than running. We started to practice, and I realized how fun it was. I left that day with the biggest smile on my face. Throughout the season, I started doing both sprints and jumps. I liked doing sprints, but the high jump was my favorite. My jumps coach wanted me to do the long jump so badly, but I hated it. I think I hated it because I was bad at it. That's why I liked the high jump because I was good at it, not the best on the team, but good enough to go to varsity meets as a freshman. I remember it was hard: We would have to go to a full sprints workout and then stay after for hours sometimes to practice high jump. I would be at track for hours each day. It was a lot, but I loved it. I loved going home and telling my mom and grandma about my new personal records (PRs).

The season was starting to come to an end and there was talk about the state championships. Me and my friend Syd were the only girl freshmen that were going to the varsity meets. We talked about how cool it would be if we both went to state, but I didn't think I would make it. It was the last meet to qualify for state. I was sitting with one of my friends that also did high jump. She was a year older, and I thought she would for sure make it to state. She was one of the better girls on the team. That meet was away, and I thought it would be my last jump of the year, so I wanted to do good. I did my jumps and felt good about them.

After you do your jumps and get out, you don't know how you scored based on a couple of factors, but in that meet, our main track coach was scoring high jump. After everyone was done jumping, I walked over with my friend to see if she made the top 3. For this meet, if you made the top 3, you went to state. She asked what she placed and sadly she didn't make it to go to state. We started to walk away when my coach asked if I wanted to know what I placed. I walked over and he told me that I placed in the top three and was going to state.

At first, it didn't register that I did it. I was going to state as a freshman! The next week, I showed up to practice and it really hit me: I was the only jumper there. I got to work one-on-one with my coach and I was starting to grow more confident. After that week of practice, I felt good, but then it was the day of the competition. I was talking with my coach when he told me he wasn't allowed over by the high jump. A rush came over me and I started to get more and more nervous.

I walked over to check in and I saw a huge group of girls that looked way more confident than I did. The first thing I noticed was they were all wearing jumping spikes and I had on my old sneakers. I didn't know anyone and was starting to feel like I wasn't good enough to be here. Then, I looked up and saw my coach on the other side of the fence with a whiteboard that said, "Breathe! You got this." A huge weight was lifted after seeing that sign.

Girls finally started jumping and everyone was making the first height, which made me start to feel nervous again. I was up next and looked out at my coach. This time the board said, "Smile." I let out a little laugh and smiled. It was finally my turn. I took a big breath in and went for it. I cleared the height! Now, my smile was a lot bigger, but I wasn't done yet. While waiting for the other girls, I kept telling myself, "I can do this."

I was up again, and a lot of girls got out on this height, but I knew I could do it. I went up and I knew I would make this height and I did. When I got off the mat, I looked up and I saw my coach showing me that I was way above the bar. Now there was only a handful of girls left. They raised the height and girls started to not make it over this one. But I knew that I was going to get this height; I wanted this. It was my turn and I made it again and got my new PR. I was so happy and surprised at the same time—I never thought I would even go to state and now I'm in the top 10.

At the next height, everyone missed but one girl and I really wanted this height. I ended up not getting it, but I was still happy about my PR. The remaining girls walked over to see what we all placed. When he read my name, it was under second place. I looked up at my coach, my mom, and my grandma and held up two fingers. They were ecstatic, and I was so happy that I did it.

That was one of the most memorable days of my life. I look back at that day when I need to remember nothing is impossible. My mindset changed after that day, I realized that you can make things happen if you believe you can. I play college soccer now and have worked hard and believed in myself through the hard times.

You will have times that are hard with injuries, mindsets, and many other things. When times get hard, I look back at that day and realize that I can do whatever I set my mind to. I've had many people tell me that I wasn't good enough to play in college and I proved them wrong and had the most goals on my team as a freshman. I knew I could do it and the more people say I'm not good enough, the more I want to prove them wrong. It's all about mindset and I know at times it can be hard, but pick a memory and remember you are strong and can do it.

~ Lexi Vernsey

The Coach

Concentrate! Fix your mind on the exact thing you desire. Close your eyes until you see its physical appearance. See yourself actually in possession of your desire.

It was a mere miracle birthed from the disaster that happened on May 16th, 2019, that my best varsity athletes, whom I coached and trained all season long to qualify for the State Championships, all completely choked in their performances at the Regional Championships. All three of my female high-jump athletes missed their last chance to win a one-way ticket to the State Championships and compete for the gold. However, one of my younger athletes seized this opportunity. A younger freshman girl I hadn't focused on or worked with all season cleared the winning height and earned a ticket to the State Championships.

I knew that this was going to be a long shot for gold. There was no possible way of conditioning her to the varsity level five days before the Championships. She was naturally athletic and mentally tough. In my professional coaching opinion, this was the recipe for building a champion.

The next day at practice, she frantically ran over to the high jump pit, and noticed she was the only athlete at high jump practice that day. Nervous and overwhelmed as she began to recreate her jump. She was shocked when I told her it didn't matter. She had a million questions, and I answered none of them.

I asked her, "What do you want to achieve?"
She said, "I want to be a champion."
I replied, "Do you believe you can?"
She answered, "I'll do anything."

I informed her that, physically, she couldn't do anything more to prepare than she already had, but, mentally, she could have whatever she wanted if her desire to win was never compromised. She nodded in agreement, and we went to work. For five days, I had her minimally jog a few laps around the track, memorize her steps, do a few jumps, then drink a couple of liters of water. At the end of her physical training sessions, we spent the rest of practice (almost one and a half hours daily) sitting down, closing her eyes, and envisioning her desire by imagining and working our way backward from becoming a champion. I called it the Envisioning Exercise.

At first, the other coaches observing my practices were concerned. They asked if I would make her sprint, hit the weight room, or focus on her technique more like they would while training their athletes for the biggest contest of the year. I chuckled each time they inquired and reassured them that this was precisely what she needed. I'm sure they all thought I was crazy. They were right. You've got to be crazy if you want to be different.

It was May 21st, 2019, the Track and Field State Championships. My freshman challenged the top competitors in the sport of the high jump. I stood behind the fence with all the other spectators with my large whiteboard sign to indicate my athlete's essentials.

As she warmed up and stretched, she looked around to soak it all in. I immediately began writing messages on my whiteboard, such as "SMILE," "Have Fun," and "Deep Breath!" Each time she read my notes, she would smile, take a breath, shrug her shoulders back, and relax.

The competition began. To our surprise, many girls couldn't clear the opening high-bar height. Lexi cleared the bar on her first jump attempt. When she jumped, it looked like she was 12 inches above the bar. She smiled, realizing that she had just set another personal record. The event continued; each competitor took their jumps. After the first round of jumps, half the competition faltered.

She jumped again in the second round, clearing the bar and looking like she had been high jumping for decades. She cheered again—another personal height record. The competition dwindled to eight athletes, including my freshman.

She took her third-round jump, gliding gracefully over the bar. As she flopped over the bar, her heel nicked the bar, causing it to leap off the stand, but it landed back into place. She had cleared her third height. ANOTHER PERSONAL RECORD!

To my excitement, three athletes remained in the final round. The high jump judge moved the bar up two more inches. I waived my whiteboard at my athlete, and again, she smiled, took a deep breath, shrugged her shoulders back, and approached her final attempt. In this final round, each girl could take a shot at the jump. Each athlete, including mine, had two missed attempts at the final height. It came down to the last jump. She sprinted, jumped her highest, flopped over the bar, and on her descent, that heel nicked the bar again, only this time, knocking the bar off the platform. She landed on the mat, threw her hands over her eyes in disappointment, and looked back at me. I already had the whiteboard waiting for her, which read, "Envision it!"

We waited for the judge to tally up the jump scores. The judge began reading off the names of the winners, starting from 8th place down to 1st. I noticed this woman and an older woman next to me intently watching Lexi. It was her mother and grandmother, just as Lexi had envisioned it at practice. Just then, the judge read my athlete's name, announcing her as the silver medalist! I danced and hugged the two ladies next to me, jumping and screaming in excitement for our girl. For a freshman to achieve what Lexi achieved, it was better than gold. She conquered the negative energy and thoughts in her mind and became a champion that day!

As she stood on top of the podium with her medal around her neck, she looked over at me, her proud coach, and mouthed the words, "I can't believe I did it." I mouthed back, "I can."

~ Jon Kovach Jr., High School Track Coach at Wasatch High School

LEXI VERNSEY

Lexi Vernsey is a college athlete and soccer player. Lexi graduated from Wasatch high school in Heber City, UT. Having competed for Wasatch soccer at the varsity level for all four years and Wasatch Track and Field, she is a competitive athlete at the elite level. With the girls' soccer program at Wasatch High School, Lexi signed to play at the next level with Salt Lake Community College. As a top goal scorer, she is tenacious and dangerous in the final 1/3. During her senior year as a captain, she played through a collarbone injury, scoring 7 goals and 2 assists, and was voted as Wasatch Fall Athlete of the Year and Varsity Team MVP.

As a track and field athlete, Lexi competed in the 100 meters, 200 meters, high jump, and long jump. Her multi-talented skill sets and strength make her a great dual threat at any track meet. Lexi is tied for the freshman record at Wasatch High School for the highest high jump cleared (4 feet 11 inches) and the highest-performing Wasatch High School athlete in the high jump at the Utah State Championships.

Lexi is currently playing college soccer at Salt Lake Community College in Utah. She is studying business and is scheduled to graduate in December of 2023 and will move on to a 4-year college, still playing soccer. During her freshman year at SLCC, she made All-Region and an All-American.

Loral Langemeier

GETTING TO "YES!" ENERGY

It is basic human nature to want to succeed in life, to dream of a better future, or just to surpass those that came before us. Nobody wants to settle, whether it's in education, the job you currently have, or where you are living.

Instead of working towards improving your life financially so that you are able to one day obtain your dream job, house, car, or lifestyle, there are too many people who would rather do nothing out of fear of failure or making a mistake.

Everyone has their own special and unique gift that makes them who they are.

Unfortunately, they are so held back by their fear of how they are perceived that they would prefer to deny their gifts altogether. In order for someone to use their gifts to their fullest potential, they need to be recognized, nurtured, and protected.

Transformation in someone occurs when they overcome these negative thoughts and transmute the energy to achieve their desires. Napoleon Hill described this as transmutation.

In my book, *Yes! Energy*, I write that, "One of the most vicious threats, deep at the core of people's failure to properly exploit their God-given gifts, is a toxic little offender called... *perfection.*"

Perfect does not exist. There are no perfect people. There is no perfect world. While, with the right energy and attitude, we can perceive everything to be perfect, trying to attain or achieve that state is a painful pursuit. Perfection is an ideal concept with no end in sight, preventing too many potential success stories from ever getting written.

Perfection does not allow for fast action or significant growth. Action is a gift. Using that gift means using energy to create, and that creation generates energy.

Part of the expense of doing business is the cost of wrong turns and mistakes. If a business or a person isn't willing to make mistakes and learn from those mistakes, there is no growth.

I try to preserve my energy by learning from the mistakes and imperfections of those who came before me. That's why I've had mentors and coaches since I was 17. I recommend always having a mentor or coach in your life. I believe in surrendering to a coach or teacher and letting that individual show me the way, instead of pursuing the route I think is perfect for me.

Life lessons occur when learning from the mistakes and imperfections of those that came before us. You should always have a mentor or a coach in your life to help maneuver through life's obstacles. There are times when you will falter, but the key is to get up, fix the problem, and learn from it. Those mistakes are there for you to learn from, so in the interim you will begin to make fewer and fewer mistakes.

In order to achieve the goals you want in life, you need to constantly change and grow. Perfectionists, however, do not like surrendering or making mistakes. Failing exposes their imperfection. In these cases, obstacles are avoided or denied, rather than confronted so they can learn from the experience and move on. Perfectionists do not pursue paths that contain obstacles, even though everything worthwhile has obstacles.

Too many live in this place of dreaming of success rather than taking a chance and seeing if it's possible. Worse, many do take a chance, fail, and crawl right back into the small place from which they came. You must fail a few times before you begin to succeed.

This stasis, this non-movement, is inaction. If action creates growth, then inaction shrinks a life.

Action is a gift. We are here to do and create. On the flip side, too many people get tangled up in a business that is not productive. People should physically embrace their imperfections. Instead, perfectionists strive to do every task as perfectly as possible but is the people who live their lives in abundance and fulfillment focus on their gifts of action and execution and cultivate an ability to perceive perfection even when everything is not quite perfect.

Our gifts are vulnerable to the attacks of outside and internal forces, which include criticism, judgement, rejection, and indifference. The ability to take criticism well is a gift.

It is also a gift to offer criticism constructively.

If you are constructively criticized, you begin to learn what is helpful as you begin to live your life and what is not. If you are scolded in such a way that is traumatic, the lesson is less productive, and the gift of learning is damaged. This goes on throughout your lifetime, as we are always learning.

The ability to learn is one of our greatest skills, especially learning in a way that fuels our energy and builds an optimistic attitude by being able to take in good criticism and deflect the hurtful and mean criticism. In turn, we need to work on our capability to offer criticism to others that benefits them on a positive level.

Constructive criticism, given or received, should begin with an acknowledgment or a positive comment. I recommend the 5:1 ratio, or five positive comments for every one criticism: "Stay away from hurtful and get to helpful."

Putting yourself out there in the world sets you up for judgement. To combat hurtful remarks, you must use your gift of tolerance—for yourself and for others.

Think about the other person's perspective and try to understand if the judgment comes from an objective place. Then you can decide how important it is for you to take on his or her judgment.

A big problem for many is that our affection for friends, partners, and family blinds us to their judgement. If you grew up in a codependent, dysfunctional family but don't even recognize that fact, then you're going to accept a lot of negative judgement that will deplete your energy and make you negative. Opening up your world to healthy people and enlightening experiences helps you find better sources of growth.

Getting rejected depletes your motivation to move forward. Getting rejected only means you move on and keep fighting. Getting rejected in either your personal or professional life feels like a personal attack. Hearing *no* is part of the process of getting to Yes! Make rejection part of the process of getting to where you want to be, but do not let rejection kill your gift.

Fortunately, you have the gift of fortitude. It feels bad to be rejected in one's personal or work life. All of it feels personal, but that feeling can be shifted with the right perspective. If you go out there and attempt to collect the *no's* in order to get to the Yes! then you make rejection part of the process.

Some might say that indifference is the cruelest attack on one's gifts. While criticism, judgment, and rejection are hurtful, they are at least active, if not negative, acknowledgments of one's gifts.

Indifference, though, is not reality for those who live in extreme energy. It only means that your gifts are being displayed in the wrong arena. The gifts of faith and certainty help us stay optimistic and energized.

When we truly recognize our gifts, we realize that these are not skills we created, but rather talents we were given and with which we were entrusted. If you truly believe in your mission and motives and are celebrating your gifts by using them, then no amount of indifference can get in your way.

If you drop your burdens, you can change the conversation to a new story. This progress, and that progress may lead to success. Plans rarely go exactly as you think they will, and success may not look the way you thought it would, but forward motion always puts you a step ahead of where you were and want to be.

Fear, guilt, shame, embarrassment, and small thinking are all adversaries that can attack our gifts and cause severe damage.

Fear, the biggest saboteur out there, preys on what we are afraid of, which includes failure, rejection, trying something new, or our fear of wasted effort or potential disappointment.

Are you really afraid of failing or are you afraid of succeeding and the enormous responsibility of success that comes with it? Even if you don't succeed, or at least don't succeed in the way you wanted, you still did something. That experience of making an effort will make the next effort that much easier. Moving forward always puts you a step ahead of where you were, even though plans rarely go exactly as you think they will, and success may not look the way you thought it would.

Many people quit when they come upon those last few troubling obstacles. If you are fully exploiting your gifts, doing all you are capable of, and blasting into extreme energy, you can stay on track.

We feel selfish or unjustified in recognizing our gifts, so we play small. You cannot help anyone else until you have helped yourself, and if you're constrained or struggling in any way, then you don't have the freedom and energy to help others. By acknowledging your gifts, you empower yourself to create abundance for yourself and those you love.

As I've mentioned before, playing small is bad for you and those around you; it serves nothing and no one. When people engage in scarcity thinking and believe that there is not enough, they fight and compete, and create fear and anxiety. If only you understood that there is more than enough for everyone, you would go get it with abandon.

Opportunity is about finding the right thing at the right time, not about numbers.

Confidence is a gift and truly believing in yourself and your gifts can overcome guilt, shame, and embarrassment. Trust yourself and your abilities. This will inspire and uplift others to do the same.

Negative criticism and harsh judgment conditions you to thinking small while playing to lose. As with external criticism and judgment, our internal criticism and judgment can attack our gifts and be a detriment to our energy and optimism. These internal messages allow us to think that we are not good enough. Not good enough to accomplish more than the average person, not good enough to stand out from the crowd, not good enough to lead, and not even good enough to have a life that goes beyond basic survival.

There are many models of what abundance and excellence look like out there, and you can learn from, and become, one of them. Even these lives don't exemplify perfection, because there is no such thing. Life can be great without being perfect.

You can lead a life as fabulous as the one you perceive someone else is having without being perfect. The gift of unlimited human potential is yours as much as it is anyone else's.

As humans, if we did not progress and grow, we would risk getting smaller and possibly evolving backward to a place of less ease and comfort, and more fear and despair. The gift of unlimited human potential must be nourished in order to attack small thinking. It begins with changing the conversation. Ask, "Why?" Don't let something be just because it has always been that way. Too many people seek permission and follow others. Living your gifts is exploiting your gifts.

When you get a progressive, exciting, energizing idea in your head, consider how that new thought got delivered into your head in the first place. Those thoughts and ideas may be gifts. It's your duty to celebrate and exploit them.

We can have abundant, fun lives that are lived responsibly. That concept is the new conversation, and it begins by shifting our view of our place in this world.

Education cannot be passive. Children shouldn't receive anything—they should dig in actively and take their education.

Let's up the education ante by changing the system, helping children think creatively and expansively, tapping into all their skills, using even their latent and unique gifts.

There is too much focus on jobs, and the expectation that most people in this world is that they will go out and get a job, because they have to have one and that they deserve one.

Jobs do not encourage people to use their God-given talents and gifts. The United States was built on the entrepreneurial spirit to create.

Thanks to our freedom, our rights, and our liberties, no one has to buy into the economy and community into which they are born. Throughout history, people have created their own microeconomies where they find their talents and gifts, and then they have traded and leveraged those skills, as well as their resources.

Interdependent entrepreneurs is a party into which anyone can invite themselves. It requires recognizing that everything is not perfect. It requires seeing a demand and creating a supply, filling a niche or void, or empowering a chain by providing a stronger link.

This perspective of the economy and community changes the conversation and allows individuals to use their gifts.

Working hard and making a lot of money is an unreal correlation. There are plenty of people who have worked hard and gotten nowhere. On the other hand, there are those who have substantial wealth and didn't break a sweat. Those who know their gifts and use their strengths do not have to work as hard as those who depend on others and do the work they are told rather than the work at which they excel.

Planning to retire is planning to die. Retirement cannot be the endgame. I switch out the term retirement for Freedom Day—a time in your life when you can do what you want, when and with whom you want. Because you can.

There are so many areas in which we fail to live up to our gifts because we are afraid of being less than perfect.

If you are going to try to do a lot in this life, you are going to be wrong sometimes. In order to even attempt to change the conversation, you are going to have to allow yourself to try out new ideas and thoughts. Opening up a dialogue only to rationalize, defend, or justify closes down the avenues of growth.

Face it: When working to achieve your goals, you are going to look stupid sometimes. When you collect experiences that create the evidence you need in order to be confident, you are going to look stupid. Being vulnerable to saying and doing stupid things helps you strengthen your gifts. It builds your lightness, your humility, and your candor, and your empathy. The best gift, in these cases, is your sense of humor.

Life can be so much bigger and better if you are willing to let go of "perfect." Allow perfect to be perception, not reality, and every day of your life will be a happy one. Let go of perfect and you will let in a lot more excitement, energy, and optimism than you ever thought possible. This will attract others, and soon you will be part of a whole new team.

LORAL LANGEMEIER

Loral Langemeier is a money expert, sought-after speaker, entrepreneurial thought leader, and bestselling author of five books. Her goal is to change the conversation people have about money worldwide and empower people to become millionaires.

The CEO and Founder of Live Out Loud, Inc.—a multinational organization—Loral relentlessly and candidly shares her best advice without hesitation or apology. What sets her apart from other wealth experts is her innate ability to recognize and acknowledge the skills & talents of people, inspiring them to generate wealth. She has created, nurtured, and perfected a 3-5 year strategy to make millions for the "Average Jill and Joe." To date, she and her team have served thousands of individuals worldwide and created hundreds of millionaires through wealth-building education keynotes, workshops, products, events, programs, and coaching services.

Loral is a money expert, Bestselling Author, and Owner & CEO of Integrated Wealth Systems—a wealth coaching company.

Growing up on her family's farm in Nebraska, Loral learned the value of hard work, persistence and how to get things done even in the face of much opposition and criticism.

Loral began her career working for the Chevron Corporation right out of college. It was clear to her early on that there was more to life than cubicles and trading her time for dollars. Despite her own fears and persuasion from friends and family against it, Loral quit her job at Chevron to become an Executive Coach.

Virtually overnight, Loral quintupled her income as an Executive Coach, while working much less. With her newfound freedom of time and accumulation of wealth she founded Live Out Loud, Inc. As a single mother, Loral has since dedicated her life to helping men and women from all walks of life to become millionaires and have time to spend with their families.

Loral's straight talk and charming personality electrifies audiences and inspires powerful action from live stages and television programs ranging from CNN, CNBC, The Street TV, Fox News Channel, Fox Business Channel-America's Nightly Scoreboard, The Dr. Phil Show, and The View. She is a regular guest-host on The Circle in Australia and has been featured in articles in USA Today, The Wall Street Journal, The New York Times, Forbes Magazine and was the breakout star in the film The Secret.

www.LoralLangemeier.com

Erik Swanson

THE FOCUS HAT TRICK

"The key to success is to focus our conscious mind on things we desire, not things we fear."
~ Brian Tracy

Transmutation? What in the heck is that? Seriously, what is it?

Okay, I think I figured it out! It took me years. But, I finally got it and can share it with you now. So many people get so confused on the term 'transmutation,' that I can understand the frustration and, more importantly, the lack of success in many people. Once you truly understand what the concept means and you follow its principle, true success is yours for the taking. In fact, you can also have a 'Hat Trick' of focus while using the principle of transmutation, as I did.

Let me explain…it's actually quite simple.

What is Transmutation?

Transmutation has a metaphorical meaning to me, in which it refers to the process of transforming or changing something fundamentally. For example, transmutation can refer to the process of transforming negative thoughts into positive ones, or turning a difficult situation into an opportunity for growth.

So, transmutation is all about change. It's about taking something and transforming it into something else entirely. And let me tell you, that's pretty awesome!

In the world of science, transmutation refers to changing one element into another by altering its atomic structure. That's right, we're talking about nuclear reactions and chemical reactions. And that's some heavy-duty stuff, let me tell you. But it's also incredibly cool and awesome if you ask me.

But transmutation isn't just limited to science. Oh no! It can also refer to transforming something on a more personal level. Maybe it's changing your negative mindset into a positive one. Maybe it's turning a difficult situation into an opportunity for growth. Whatever it is, transmutation is about taking what you have and making it even better.

Transmutation and Focus

For many people around the world, it sometimes becomes a task to simply focus in on a specific area. For years upon years, psychologists have been studying the effects of 'focus' in people. They study and try to identify the best strategies humans use to have the best results when focusing on a single area.

My main mentor in my self-development life, Brian Tracy, used to personally train me how to use what he calls "single handling." Single handling is when you train your mind and commit to only focusing on one area for a certain time period. For example, you say to yourself you will commit the next 90 minutes to completing a certain task. You must commit and don't deviate from the task. Once you complete the task, you can set up a reward that you have completed it, such as going for a walk or grabbing a bite to eat.

I have done my own exhaustive studies in this area as well. What I have found is that when I use transmutation along with my single handling focus, I am immensely more successful in my ultimate outcome. Single handling focus is great, but implementing the transmutation concept into the equation yields much better results for long-term success.

The Speed of Success Using Transmutation

When consciously attended to, success in any area of your life is much easier to accomplish when attached to an ultimate outcome. It's even easier when not only attached to an ultimate outcome, but also giving meaning to the 'release' of certain areas that are not desired in your life anymore that does not serve a purpose. And, even easier and faster results are achieved when those areas you wish to delete out of your life are transmuted or changed into a positive area in which you desire to achieve and make into a habit for life.

3 Major Areas I Transmuted Out of My Life:

I make a conscious decision to transmute 3 areas of my life into 3 amazing success areas. It's one thing to consciously decide to delete something out of your life. But it's another amazing concept to use the principle of transmuting in which you change or replace an area with another positive area. Here are 3 areas that had a huge impact in my life.

1. **I QUIT DRINKING COFFEE!** I decided to take coffee off the table for myself. The reason behind this was simple. I kept finding myself reaching for a cup of coffee before I could do anything else in the mornings. This was becoming an issue. I found it funny that I made a habit of having to rely on something outside of my control. After seriously thinking about it, I decided to replace coffee with green iced tea so that it would be healthier for me and not give me as much caffeine. More importantly, I wanted to break the habit of having to rely on something each morning. I transmuted coffee into green iced tea and also decided that I would actually be 'coffee' for others in helping them be positive each and every morning; not only coffee for them, but espresso!

2. **I QUIT DRINKING ALCOHOL!** I decided to quit drinking alcohol all-together. This was literally one of the best decisions I have ever made in my life. I started to notice that I really wasn't myself after I had a drink or two. In fact, I started to notice my friends would start to ignore my phone calls when I tried reaching out to them. It wasn't until a good friend of mine, who was featured in the movie and book The Secret and a celebrity author in our book series in The 13 Steps to Riches, John Assaraf, mentioned to me when we were out to dinner one night that he loves me, but doesn't love hanging around me when I've been drinking. He explained that I'm a great human, but a different human when I introduce alcohol into the situation. Right then and there, I decided I was done with that. I was done with something that didn't serve me at all. I decided to transmute my time and energy from drinking alcohol to writing books. Yes, like this book you are holding in your hands right now! Wow, what an amazing transmutation! I am now a 13-time #1 Bestselling Author and have created 5 separate #1 bestselling book series with over 120 clients as #1 Bestselling Authors in my series now. Wow!

3. **I QUIT NEGATIVITY!** I decided to make a conscious decision to get rid of negativity in my life. In exchange I would transmute any negative thoughts into positive, awesome thoughts. This also changed my life! Our friend Deepak Chopra used to ask us if we were allowing other people to rent space in our minds with their negative thoughts. He explained that we were probably not even charging them rent for it either. Why allow negative thoughts into our minds? Why allow these negative thoughts to sit and fester inside of us like weeds in a garden? These thoughts or weeds will take over the whole landscape if we allow it to. I made a decision to transmute any negative thoughts into awesome thoughts and help others around me see that they, too, can change their mindset. This was the genesis of my motto which I call, "NDSO!" This stands for "No Drama, Serve Others!"

So, whether you're talking about changing elements or changing yourself, transmutation is all about transformation. And if you ask me, that's pretty darn awesome! So go out there and transmute! Make something awesome! Create your own "Focus Hat Trick" and see how your life will change for the better. You deserve it.

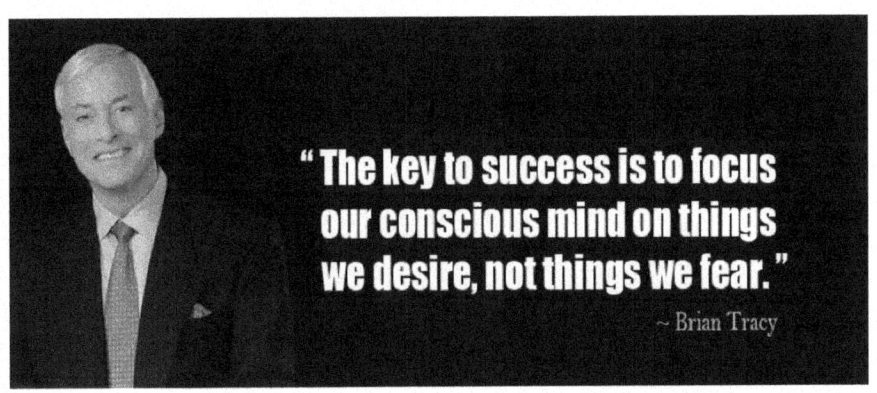

"The key to success is to focus our conscious mind on things we desire, not things we fear."

~ Brian Tracy

ERIK SWANSON

As an Award-Winning International Keynote Speaker and Multi Time #1 International Bestselling Author, Erik "Mr. Awesome" Swanson is in great demand around the world! He speaks to an average of more than one million people per year. Mr. Swanson has the honor to have been invited to speak to many schools around the world including the prestigious Harvard University. He is also a recurring Faculty Member of CEO Space International as well as an Alumni Keynoter at Vistage Executive Coaching. Erik's speeches can be found on Amazon Prime TV as well as joining the Ted Talk Family with his latest speech called, "A Dose of Awesome."

Erik got his start in the self-development world by mentoring directly under Brian Tracy. Quickly climbing to become the top trainer around the world from a group of over 250 handpicked coaches, Erik started to surround himself with the best of the best and very quickly started to be invited to speak on stages alongside such greats as Jim Rohn, Bob Proctor, Les Brown, Sharon Lechter, Jack Canfield, Lisa Nichols, and Joe Dispenza—just to name a few. Erik has created and developed the super-popular Habitude Warrior Conference, which has a two-year waiting list and includes 33 top-named speakers from around the world. It is a 'Ted Talk' style event which has quickly climbed to one of the top 10 events not to miss in the United States! He is the creator, founder, and CEO of the Habitude Warrior Mastermind and Global Speakers Mastermind. He is also the creator and publisher of *The 13 Steps To Riches* book series as well as *The Principles of David & Goliath* book series. His motto is clear: "NDSO!": No Drama – Serve Others!

www.SpeakerErikSwanson.com

Jon Kovach Jr.

THE ENERGY ABUNDANCE

There are many powerful motivators in life. On the positive side, decision, motivation, inspiration, desire, faith, hope, charity, understanding, clarity, fun, intuition, and leadership are all powerful motivators. On the negative side, fear, doubt, frustration, disbelief, anger, sadness, manipulation, abuse, betrayal, and revenge can have the same motivational powers. All these motivators derive from believing you are either deserving or undeserving. Many incredible outcomes have been acquired and achieved through any one of these potential energies.

I am not ashamed to say that I have experienced many positive and negative motivators. I believe it's only natural for any human to experience each of these in some way. Significantly, what you do with each experience ultimately transforms your future.

I didn't realize it then, but a new energy was born when I decided to hang up my track and field spikes and walk away from the sport. Through my personal experiences, professional dedication, and physical transformations, I have learned the principles of Transmutation and inner-power control. I converted my energy into a whole new world of results.

I've been told by many who have interviewed me and have appeared on stage with me that I have lived an extraordinary life in my short 30-something years, more than the average person does their entire life. I've accomplished a great deal in my short life, from physical and athletic transformations to spiritual and ecclesiastical devotions. From an inexperienced lemonade stand entrepreneur to the owner of two high-performing high-ticket businesses, I have found a way to convert my physical energy as an elite athlete into the energy of a high-performance entrepreneur.

At a young age, I chose not to wait. Call it impatience, if you will, but my ADHD has become a superpower in controlling my energy and focusing my brain. I've felt first-hand the concentration of harnessing mother nature's most remarkable powers. If you're keeping score, you'll know that mother nature has never lost. She's 100% uncontested. Her powers and abilities are unmatched and have faced no worthy opponent. When you trust nature's forces and laws, you can harness mother nature's power, access higher power, and exude the energy of a winner and champion. This means that your natural functions and abilities are your most incredible superpowers, even if your innate nature includes modern-day socially deemed challenges, deficits, impediments, or unique diagnoses.

Faster Than A Speeding Bullet

For me, the power of Transmutation is converting one motivational energy into another. That power can be positive or negative. For example, while playing basketball, I remember getting fouled by an opponent, resulting in a fist to my face. Physically, I turned to anger and frustration. The anger motivated me to return to the court and score several points, putting our team back in the lead. Positively, my anger fueled my physical drive to achieve more.

However, the frustration countered my anger with unpredictable behavior and turned me into a fouling Tasmanian devil—I was out of control. Although I accomplished the first objective, to outscore our opponent and get us back into the lead, amid my tornado-like behavior, I also managed to foul out of the game.

We lost that game anyway. I am not one of those coaches and leaders who say everything is rainbows and roses, but I want you to recognize that a lot of good can come from adverse events. Controlling negativity prevents the spiral decline of behavior. I want you to understand that positive energy motivators such as joy and laughter can become your greatest energy source, just like in the Disney Pixar animated film *Monsters Inc*. Rather than fear being the most significant source of power and energy to the monster world, positivity is greater and more sustainable and controllable in all our lives.

Here's another sports example that shows the epitome of my athleticism versus my energy response motivators. While playing football at the varsity level, I had a habit of reading the quarterbacks' eyes. At the same time, I was on defense and falling for their fake moves, leaving me vulnerable and a wide-open receiver downfield to catch the ball uncontested and run for a touchdown. My number one role as the strong safety of the football team was to keep the ball in front of me and to prevent anyone from entering the end zone. I knew that I was the fastest person on any field. I could outrun anybody and last longer than anyone else.

However, when I made that mistake and fell for fake plays, my opponent, whom I was supposed to defend, would catch the football and run for a touchdown. Knowing I had made a mistake and fearing I'd let them score, I used that negative motivator to give me physical fuel-power and turn on my hyper-speed jets in my legs, chasing down the opponents and tackling them before they could score. Although my coaches were extremely frustrated with these mistakes, they were always equally grateful that I prevented the score from happening.

My father would joke about me at church while speaking at the pulpit. He'd share the powerful lesson of realization and forgiveness and use the stories of my mistakes to relate to the congregation. He'd share from his spectator's perspective, watching me realize that I made a mistake, slapping my helmet in frustration, then turning on the jet boosters and making the tackle anyway. Seeing this young man transform his body into a speeding bullet was an entertaining spectacle for many eyes. It's a relatable lesson for all that a negative motivator can work in transmuting energy into positive results.

The Cave People Theory

Many people are familiar with the concept of cavemen, cavewomen, and Neanderthals. It is understood that these cave people lived off necessities, had limited cognitive power and ability, and ultimately knew what to do and how to survive. Any animal in any part of the food chain or ecosystem knows how to survive. A caveman's paternal power was to leave the cave, find food, hunt, drag food back to the cave, close it for safety, and feed their family. An essential skill set is a natural fight-or-flight response to the necessity to survive. The positive energy motivator of survival leads any caveman to do precisely what is necessary to achieve their goals—stay alive.

The tremendous maternal powerful motivator of the cavewoman was a combination of nature and nurture. While they would accompany the caveman in the hunting and gathering duties, a more significant source of power was given to the cavewoman in balancing survival and creation. Giving birth and nurturing the family became a necessity and a natural nesting instinct of any mammal. These two powers combined lead to the building of communities, civilizations, and species' growth.

In the modern day, we still aren't too far off from those natural cave people's instincts. The moment I met my wife, I knew I couldn't survive without her. I did everything naturally possible to continue to serve, attract, and maintain a relationship and status with her. A romantic story began on a bus trip across the Midwest, where I started to develop our long-term loving relationship. Even when she expressed the desire to live abroad and teach English in Russia through a school program, I needed to maintain that connection, and survival skills turned into overdrive.

To not let the flame burn out, I tried to be continually impressive and romantic and stayed in touch through Skype and FaceTime while she was abroad. Our constant communication and connection only depended on our love for each other, and we made an effortless transition when she returned home from her trip. That paternal instinct dates to the original beings. I'm grateful for those natural powers and how they motivated me to continue to be with my wife and love her.

Love and passion are great motivators as well. February 20, 2016, the night my mom got the call that she would receive a new pair of lungs through transplant surgery, she informed all of the family that she loved her children and family and that we meant everything to her. Hundreds of miles away, I drove day and night to get there by the time she was out of surgery and be there for her as she entered the world with a new pair of lungs.

Her body was extremely swollen and filled with tubes and medications. She was incapacitated and unconscious, resting from the traumatic procedure. But that didn't change my love and passion for serving her, even if she didn't know I was there. I reached out to her swollen foot and tried massaging it so she could feel slightly less uncomfortable. After rubbing her foot, there was no response or reaction for about 20 minutes, and I took a small break to rest my hands. Immediately, the foot that I had been massaging started to kick my hand, nudging it as if it was encouraging me to continue massaging.

I looked up at my still, motionless mom and realized she was communicating with me. I continued rubbing her feet for the next hour, and after I had finished, I looked up again at the unconscious woman and saw a subtle smile. I knew that our love was there and still alive. This moment was one of the greatest memories that has impacted my relationship and love for my mom.

Six years later, on October 28, 2022, my mom lay again on the ever-familiar hospital bed, taking her last breaths. As I massaged her swollen hands and feet like before, her pain and discomfort slowly slipped away. Our connection as mother and son was pure love in those final moments. I'm forever grateful for our powerful bond during those scary moments. I can testify of the transmutative power that turned the horrifying event of losing my mom into one of the most positive experiences in my life. I believe that my mom and I converted an overwhelming amount of negativity and sadness into a positive, powerful energy for a moment unfathomable.

Whether in athletics, entrepreneurship, public speaking, coaching, or simply sharing love with others, all humans can harness mother nature's power and convert any source of energy into an even greater outcome. As I mentioned before, my peers have told me that I've lived multiple lives in my few years, and I would attribute that to my ability to use transmutative power to do things that most people wouldn't do. My restlessness and ADHD have fueled my mind and body to get off the couch and experience life fully.

Even in slumber, rest, or inaction, I was productively in action. As an athlete, I learned that:

Resistance + Rest = Growth and Strength.

The heart and soul need productive action and rest to grow.

Alexander Hamilton shared his frustration with dissatisfaction as depicted in the Broadway musical named after him. His motivator in life was that he would never be satisfied.

George Washington knew the nation would never grow to be what it was until he stepped down as President of the United States and allowed the system they created to give life to a new leader.

Socrates died for what he believed in, so he willingly went to his death, knowing that his work led to the development and evolution of modern-day foundations for philosophy.

The Beatles became one of the greatest bands in history, arguably altering pop, rock, and many other genres of music that branched from the foundation of the music they created. Many decades later, the Beatles' songs are still on the radio as relevant music, and even stations are dedicated to their work.

Also, many decades later, it is still a conversation of debate whether **Michael Jordan** is still the greatest basketball player ever to play the game.

The Nobel Peace Prize has evolved from some of the greatest inventions ever created to some of the most fantastic theories, methodologies, and solutions to human rights and the philosophies of freedom.

Just like in the example of mother nature, the world is going through its own Transmutation, converting the energy from one generation to another. The world carries the legacy of the giants on whose shoulders we currently stand, and we pave a new path for future generations. A restoration of energy, atmosphere, environment, ecosystem, and balance are presently in effect.

I encourage you to use strategic rest methods to harness the powers of Transmutation. I call this the great recharge. The more you know yourself, your body, and your beliefs, the more you know what it takes to recharge you after stress, activity, and physical action. Here's a list of ways that I use rest to restore at an accelerated rate so that I can transmit more energy for success for desire.

Accelerated Methods to Recharge: stretching, yoga, breathing exercises, resistance training, reading, affirmations and declarations, access to nature, walking barefoot through the grass, sitting or lying in a river, ice baths, swimming, spa days, breath exercises, adventure, travel, embracing emotions, writing, journaling, breaks from blue light and screens, research and learning, reading books, going to the library, fresh air, adventures, adrenaline rushes, exposure to animals in nature, walking through sand, drinking fresh, cool, water, meditation, spinal movements, hip and joint movement, massage, foods rich in spices, unprocessed produce, fresh fruits and vegetables, fasting, fasting from sugar, dancing, music, singing loudly to music, smiling, barking like a dog, power, poses, reaching for the sky, humor, laughter, micro muscle movements, talking to myself, and talking to enthusiastic and positive people—to name a few.

Each of these methods is an excellent tool for recharging your mind, body, and soul to quickly get back to activity, production, and harnessing the power of Transmutation in your life. I've learned and believe that any human's primary drive is meaning, vitality, belonging, validation, and progress.

One of my favorite scenes in any movie is Disney's *Rocketman*, where the commander crashes the Mars Vehicle and is pinned underneath it on Martian soil. His companion at the time, Fred, doesn't panic but tells the commander to call him mommy. Fred looks at the commander in the eyes and says, "Quick commander, they say a mother can summon the power of twenty men when her child is in duress. Quick, call me mommy!" The commander looks at Fred and says, "I'd rather die on the Martian turf!" Fred doesn't except his answer and says, "Come on commander, call me, mommy!" The commander reluctantly whimpers, "Mommy, mommy, please save me, mommy...."

Fred receives the message, summons the power of twenty men, and screams at the top of his lungs, "Mommy's coming, little Billy!" And Fred lifts the Martian rover just enough, allowing the commander to slide out from underneath its grasp. Saving the commander in one movement, he drops the rover on the ground. Both escape just in time to reach the spaceship before a Martian storm swallows them up. This example shows how transmutative power converts duress into superhuman strength.

Acquiring access to these higher, natural powers is not unrealistic. I challenge you to be disciplined in your decisions and focus on active progress.

> *"You may not be done, but you can be complete. You may not be satisfied, but you could be fulfilled. You may not have won t he battle, but the war isn't over."*
> ~ Jon Kovach Jr.

Any amount of resistance, followed by a recharge, will give you the exact formula for harnessing the power of Transmutation and turning any desire into its physical equivalent. Here's my invitation to show up and stand in your greatness. Everything you need is within you now!

JON KOVACH JR

About Jon Kovach Jr.: Jon is an award-winning international motivational speaker and global mastermind leader. Jon has helped multi-billion-dollar corporations exceed their annual sales goals, including Coldwell Banker Commercial, Outdoor Retailer Cotopaxi, and the Public Relations Student Society of America. In addition, in his work as an accountability coach and mastermind facilitator, Jon has helped thousands of professionals overcome their challenges and achieve their goals by implementing his accountability strategies and Irrefutable Laws of High Performance. Jon is the Founder and Chairman of Champion Circle. Jon is the Mastermind Facilitator and Team Lead of the Habitude Warrior Mastermind and the Global Speakers Mastermind & Masterclass founded by Speaker Erik "Mr. Awesome" Swanson.

Jon speaks on topics including accountability, The Irrefutable Laws of High Performance, and The Power of Mastermind Methodologies. He is a #1 Bestselling Author and a featured keynote on SpeakUp TV, an Amazon Prime TV series, with his keynote speech titled, Getting Unstuck. In addition, he stars in over 100 speaking stages, podcasts, and live international summits each year. Jon's motivational messages have been viewed by over 500,000 people online. His positive messages have trended and been used by global brands on TikTok and Instagram, such as: Red Bull, Michael Bublé, NHL, Powell Books, GoDaddy Studio, Canada's Wonderland Amusement Park, and the LSU Cheer Team.

Author's website: *www.SpeakerJonKovachJr.com*

Book Series Website: *www.TheBookofInfluence.com*

Amado Hernandez

A MI QUERIDA CALEÑA ADRIANA HESFORD

"Once upon a time, in a faraway land, a young prince lived in a shining castle. Although he had everything his heart desired, the prince was spoiled, selfish, and unkind. But then, one winter's night, an old beggar woman came to the castle and offered him a single rose in exchange for shelter from the bitter cold. Repulsed by her haggard appearance, the prince sneered at the gift and turned the old woman away, but she warned him not to be deceived by appearances, for beauty is found from within. And when he dismissed her again, the old woman's ugliness melted away to reveal a beautiful enchantress. The prince tried to apologize, but it was too late, for she had seen that there was no love in his heart. And, as punishment, she transformed him into a hideous beast and placed a spell on the castle and all who lived there.

Ashamed of his monstrous form, the beast concealed himself inside his castle, with a magic mirror as his only window to the outside world. The rose she offered was truly enchanted and would bloom until his 21st year. If he could learn to love another and earn her love in return by the time the last petal fell, the spell would be broken. If not, he would be doomed to remain a beast forever. As the years passed, he fell into despair and lost all hope—for who could ever learn to love a beast?"

By now, you're wondering what the opening monologue from *Beauty and the Beast* has to do with *The Power of Transmutation* as described by Napoleon Hill. Like me, you've probably read Napoleon Hill's *Think and Grow Rich* and maybe even *The Law of Success*. So, I am not going to simply restate or attempt to explain Mr. Hill's concept, but I will comment that "transmutation" is an ageless and powerful universal law. And it's a concept that has been effectively used intentionally and unintentionally since the beginning of time. Understanding and mastering the power of transmutation has infinite benefits and unlimited applications.

Back to *Beauty and the Beast*. If you know the story, you'll remember that the beast was given a one-time, limited opportunity to transform himself from a hideous monster back into prince charming. How did he do this? The prince used transmutation long before Napoleon Hill introduced its powers and principles to us. *Beauty and the Beast* was written in 1749 by French author Gabrielle Suzanne de Villeneuve. The plot of the original fairy tale differs significantly from Walt Disney's 1991 movie.

In all written and film versions of *Beauty and the Beast*, including the 2012-2016 TV series, the prince who had been transformed into a monster is confronted by a dilemma when Belle is introduced into the plot. He had to choose between negativity and love. In the classic "damsel in distress" scenario, the Beast could have kept Belle in her prison cell and would have sabotaged all chances of transforming himself back into a handsome prince. Instead, the Beast employed "transmutation" to channel his energy to learning to love and accept himself, love Belle, and earn Belle's love in return. Hill referred to love as "the amplifier of energy." Beast amplified his positive energy and transmuted negativity into love.

This may be the only time you'll hear of this connection between *Beauty and the Beast* and transmutation. But think about it! It's simple and reasonable. How else could the Beast have been able to achieve the goal of transforming himself back into Prince through positive focused energy? "For who could ever learn to love a beast?"

When Napoleon Hill introduced the power of transmutation in 1937, Hill tackled the radical topic that would become the most powerful, and yet, the least discussed of all of his teachings. Liken this to someone suggesting you look directly at the sun, knowing you may start seeing black dots for a while.

Born in Los Angeles in 1921, Earl Nightingale V was 16 in 1937 when he read *Think and Grow Rich* (about the same age at which I first read the book). Nightingale went on to become a powerful and successful radio personality and author focusing on human character development, motivation, and meaningful lifestyles. Long before Tony Robbins rose to prominence, Nightingale was known as the "Dean of Personal Development." In 1960 Nightingale recorded a narrated and condensed version of *Think and Grow Rich* and changed Hill's original chapter on transmutation to *The Power of Enthusiasm*. Transmutation is power and enthusiastic energy.

Let's think about transmutation in its practical applications. Transmutation had to have had a role in the successes of all famous entertainers, athletes, innovators, and influencers, from Madonna to Lady Gaga, from Michael Jackson to Michael Jordan, and from Meat Loaf to Snoop Dogg. No one knows the actual nature, level, or degree of the power of transmutation anyone employs, but we can assume that everyone who has reached fame and fortune has used it successfully.

And that brings us to you. Are you a Beauty or a Beast? We're not talking about physically—we're talking about spiritually. Do you fall asleep each night and wake up each morning loving yourself, able to accept and cherish being loved, and positively capable of loving others?

One morning a traveling salesman woke up to find himself transformed into a large insect. That's what happened to Gregor Samsa in *The Metamorphosis* by Frank Kafka. Maybe that's you trying to wake up after this pandemic nightmare we've been going through. Samsa looked around his room, and everything looked normal, so he pulled the covers over his head and tried to go back to sleep. But realizing he had many more legs that he went to bed with and a disgusting body, he reflected on his dreary life. Sadly, the story ends with Gregor being unable to change himself back into his prior physical body and eventually dying.

Don't allow yourself to be a Gregor Samsa, a miserable insect hiding and waiting to die. Think of the other beasts that used the power of transmutation to transform themselves back into Prince or Princess.

Thanks to the courage and wisdom of Napoleon Hill, we understand the power of positive energy that can be channeled into our personal development and reaching our goals.

AMADO HERNANDEZ

About Amado Hernandez: About Amado Hernandez: Amado was born in Mexico of humble beginnings and raised in Los Angeles, California. As an avid reader, Amado always focused on self-development. He coaches sales professionals to make six and seven figures in real estate.

Amado believes in a progressive culture, a people-centric culture where clients' dreams come true and salespeople thrive; at the end of the day, we all want to be respected and pursue our happiness. My goal is to leave a legacy-making a difference in people's lives.

With 35 years of Real Estate experience, Mr. ABC Amado Hernandez successfully operates and grows his Excellence Empire Real Estate Moreno Valley office. Broker/Owner Amado first opened his doors in 1995, and Excellence currently has over 60 offices in Southern California, Las Vegas, Merida Yucatan, Mexico, and over 1,000 Agents. He is also part owner of a highly successful Mortgage company, Excellence Mortgage, and owner of Empire Escrow Services. Mr. Amado is also involved with his community and currently serves as Director at Inland Valley Association of Realtors (IVAR) and will be the President for 2023. Amado serves as a Director of CAR (California Association of Realtors).

Author's Website: *www.ExcellenceEmpireRE.com*

Book Series Website & Author's Bio: *www.The13StepsToRiches.com*

Angelika Ullsperger

REDIRECTING THOUGHTS & EMOTIONS

How can we use transmutation to achieve a higher level of success? Well, first, we must understand what transmutation is and how it works before we can look at it in action. Napolean Hill defines transmutation as the process of converting negative thoughts and emotions into positive ones and notes that this process is an important key to success.

The first step in the process of transmutation, according to Hill, is to acknowledge negative thoughts and emotions. He advises against denying or suppressing them, as this can lead to them becoming stronger and more pervasive. Instead, he suggests that individuals should confront their negative thoughts and emotions head-on, examine their origins, and try to understand why they are experiencing them.

The second step in the process of transmutation is to replace negative thoughts and emotions with positive ones. Hill suggests using affirmations, visualization, and positive self-talk to achieve this. Affirmations are statements that individuals repeat to themselves to reinforce positive beliefs and behaviors. Visualization involves mentally imagining oneself achieving their goals and experiencing positive emotions. Positive self-talk is the practice of consciously directing one's thoughts in a positive direction.

Hill emphasizes that the process of transmutation requires persistence and repetition. It takes time and effort to change ingrained patterns of negative thinking and behavior. However, he also notes that the rewards of transmutation are significant. By converting negative thoughts and emotions into positive ones, individuals can harness their energy and creativity, leading to greater success in all areas of their lives.

Hill cites many examples of individuals who have successfully used the process of transmutation to achieve success. For example, Andrew Carnegie, who rose from humble beginnings to become one of the wealthiest individuals in the world. Carnegie attributed his success to his ability to transmute negative thoughts and emotions into positive ones, which allowed him to focus on his goals and achieve them.

The concept of transmutation is a powerful tool for achieving success. By acknowledging and confronting negative thoughts and emotions and replacing them with positive ones, individuals can harness their energy and creativity to achieve their goals. While the process of transmutation requires persistence and effort, the rewards are significant, as evidenced by the many successful individuals who have used this technique to achieve their dreams.

So, let's explore this idea by taking a look at the story of my friend, Sarah.

Sarah had a dream of starting her own business. She had a life-long passion for baking, and she yearned to open a bakery that offered unique and delicious treats. Opening this bakery had been her dream since childhood.

However, for as long as she could remember, she worked jobs she hated just to get by. Sarah was plagued by many negative thoughts and emotions that held her back. She was afraid that her business would fail, and she worried that she wasn't skilled enough to make her dream a reality. All of these thoughts weighed on her, making it difficult for her to take action and move forward with her plans.

One day, Sarah came across *Think and Grow Rich* and the concept of transmutation. The idea of converting negative thoughts and emotions into positive ones intrigued her, and she decided to give it a try.

At first, it was hard for Sarah to confront her negative thoughts and emotions. She found herself feeling overwhelmed by her fears and doubts. Oftentimes, she wanted to give up. However, as she persisted in her efforts, she began to notice a change.

Instead of feeling paralyzed by her negative thoughts, Sarah began to feel more energized and motivated. She started to see her fears and doubts as challenges that she could overcome, rather than obstacles that would hold her back.

Sarah also began using affirmations, visualization, and positive self-talk to reinforce her positive beliefs and behaviors. She repeated to herself that she was capable of starting a successful bakery, and she visualized herself running a thriving business. She also directed her thoughts in a positive direction, focusing on the steps she needed to take to make her dream a reality.

Over time, Sarah's efforts paid off. She was able to secure funding for her business, and she opened her bakery to much success. Her unique and delicious treats quickly gained a following, and she found herself busy with orders and customers.

Looking back, Sarah realized that the process of transmutation had been essential to her success. By confronting and converting her negative thoughts and emotions into positive ones, she was able to overcome her fears and doubts and make her dream a reality.

From that point on, Sarah continued to use the process of transmutation to overcome any challenges that came her way. She became a successful business owner, and her bakery became a beloved part of the community. Her story serves as a reminder that with persistence and effort, anyone can achieve their dreams by harnessing the power of transmutation.

Brain plasticity refers to the brain's ability to change and adapt in response to experiences, learning, and behavior. This concept is based on the idea that the brain is not fixed or unchangeable, but rather malleable and capable of forming new neural connections throughout one's lifetime.

So, what concepts are behind the magic of transmutation?

One of the key aspects is neuroplasticity. Neuroplasticity is the brain's ability to change its physical structure in response to new experiences, learning, and behavior. Neuroplasticity allows the brain to form new connections between neurons and to strengthen existing connections, enabling us to learn new skills, change our behavior, and adapt to new situations.

The concept of transmutation is, in part, based on the principles of neuroplasticity. By consciously redirecting our thoughts and emotions towards positive ones, we can create new neural pathways that reinforce positive beliefs and behaviors.

For example, when we practice affirmations or positive self-talk, we are actively stimulating the prefrontal cortex, the part of the brain responsible for executive functioning, decision-making, and emotional regulation. The repetition of positive statements creates new neural connections in the prefrontal cortex, strengthening our ability to regulate our emotions and make positive decisions.

Similarly, visualization is a powerful tool for harnessing the brain's plasticity. When we visualize ourselves achieving a desired outcome, we activate the same neural networks that would be activated if we were actually performing the action. This helps to reinforce the neural connections associated with the behavior we want to develop, making it easier for us to perform the action in real life.

Finally, the process of transmutation is also based on the principle of cognitive reappraisal, which involves reinterpreting a situation or emotion in a positive way. This technique is based on the idea that the brain's emotional response to a situation is influenced by the way we interpret it. By consciously reframing negative situations in a positive light, we can change the way our brain responds to them, reducing feelings of stress and anxiety.

In summary, the concept of transmutation works because it is based on the principles of brain plasticity and neuroplasticity. By consciously redirecting our thoughts and emotions towards positive ones, we can create new neural pathways that reinforce positive beliefs and behaviors. This helps us to regulate our emotions, make positive decisions, and achieve our goals, ultimately leading to greater success and happiness.

ANGELIKA ULLSPERGER

About Angelika Ullsperger: Angelika is a serial entrepreneur from Baltimore, Maryland. She is a fashion designer, model, artist, photographer, and musician. Angelika has extensive and well-rounded professional experience, having worked as a business owner, carpenter, chef, graphic designer, manager, event planner, sales and product specialist, marketer, and coach. Angelika is now a #1 Bestselling Author in the historic book series, *The 13 Steps to Riches*. She is a life-long learner with a sincere and genuine interest in all things of the world with a major interest in the formal subject of abnormal psychology, neuroscience, and quantum physics.

Angelika prides herself as someone who has saved lives as a friend, first responder, EMT, and knowledgeable suicide prevention advocate. With a vast knowledge and experience in multiple professions, Angelika is also a proud honorable member of Phi Theta Kappa, The APA, the AAAS, and an FBLA (Future Business Leaders Association) Business Competition Finalist. She is Certified in basic coding and blockchain technology. Amongst the careers and vast experience, Angelika is an adventurer and avid dog lover.

Her ultimate goals and dreams are to make a lasting positive impact in people's lives through her wealth of knowledge and skillsets.

Author's Website: *www.Angelika.world*

Book Series Website & Author's Bio: *www.The13StepsToRiches.com*

Anthony M. Criniti IV

THE MYSTERY OF SURVIVAL ESSENTIALS TRANSMUTATION

Think and Grow Rich by Napoleon Hill is one of the best classic books to teach someone about how to become a financial success (as well as a success in other areas of life). In there, you will find his thirteen steps to riches; each has a separate chapter and analysis. The subject of our book is to interpret his tenth step to riches: *The Mystery of Sex Transmutation*. Let's review some of the major highlights of this chapter, which we will refer to as *The Power of Transmutation and Energy*.

At first glance, it is easy to feel confused with this apparently odd chapter title in *Think and Grow Rich*. You might ask yourself: How could a topic that is so taboo properly fit into the context of a book like this? To answer this question, let's start with what Hill meant by transmutation. Hill explains: "Transmutation is simple and easily explained. It means the switching of the mind from thoughts of physical expression to thoughts of some other nature" (Hill, 2011, p. 263).

Many individuals, particularly men, wasted their whole life hunting for partners. This time they spent would not be regained; hence, their real talents and wealth were never fully maximized. The high cost of time lost was the price paid for the persistent pursuit of personal pleasure. As stated in Principle 184 of *The Most Important Lessons in Economics and*

Finance: "Sexual obsession leads to wealth depression" (Criniti, 2014, p. 217).

On the other hand, people who can control and redirect their natural physical desires into a more productive outlet will have a higher probability of fulfilling their talents. The greatest leaders in history could collect and contain their physical energy and force it to travel toward their creation. Hill states that physical "energy is the creative energy of all genius. There never has been, and never will be, a great leader, builder, or artist lacking in this driving force" (Hill, 2011, p. 275).

Further, Hill elaborates on the secrets of the genius: "Fortunate, indeed, is the person who has discovered how to give...emotion an outlet through some form of creative effort, for he has, by that discovery, lifted himself to the status of the genius. Scientific research has disclosed these significant facts: 1. The men of greatest achievement are men with highly developed sex natures, men who have learned the art of transmutation. 2. The men who have accumulated great fortunes and achieved outstanding recognition in literature, art, industry, architecture, and the professions, were motivated by the influence of [attraction]" (Hill, 2011, p. 264-265).

In this chapter, there was also a connection made between energy transmutation, emotions, and our future. Once you understand the importance of emotional intelligence, you can positively change how you view life. Since Hill considers the powers of positive emotions, knowing how to control emotion can bring someone life-changing consequences. Hill states: "The emotions are states of mind. Nature has provided man with a "chemistry of the mind" which operates in a manner similar to the principles of chemistry of matter" (Hill, 2011, p. 285).

Your attitude towards a particular subject can determine your specific feelings towards it. This can then determine whether or not you will be successful in implementing its principles. For example, the majority of the planet does not excel in finance because of their negative perspective of it.

However, as stated in *The Necessity of Finance*: "If finance is one of the most important subjects that exist, it should not be classified as boring" (Criniti, 2013, p. 59). How could people be successful in building wealth if their emotional compass is pointing in the wrong direction?

How important are the right emotions? According to Hill: "The world is ruled, and the destiny of civilization is established by the human emotions. People are influenced in their actions, not by reason so much as by "feelings." The creative faculty of the mind is set into action entirely by emotions and not by cold reason" (Hill, 2011, p. 278).

From a practical side, if you agree with what has been said so far, you can immediately implement this knowledge by shifting your paradigm of the sales process. This knowledge can help people properly manage the influence that others have on them and realize why they may or may not have an influence on others.

Hill elaborates on how people are influenced: "The public speaker, orator, preacher, lawyer, or salesman lacking in [attraction] energy is a "flop," as far as being able to influence others is concerned. Couple this with the fact that most people can be influenced only by appealing to their emotions, and you will understand the importance of [attraction] energy as a part of the salesman's native ability. Master salesmen attain the status of mastery in selling because they, consciously or unconsciously, transmute the energy of [attraction] into sales enthusiasm! This statement may be a very practical suggestion as to the meaning of... transmutation" (Hill, 2011, p. 279-280).

Another interesting part of this chapter was Hill's view on the relationship between men, women, and wealth. In short, women have been the carrot on the end of a stick, enticing men to be successful throughout history. If you extend his logic out a few notches, it is easy to conclude that civilization might not have occurred at all, let alone reached the present level, if men did not desire to please women.

Hill explains: "Man has the same desire to please women that he had before the dawn of civilization. The only thing that has changed is his method of pleasing. Men who accumulate large fortunes, and attain great heights of power and fame, do so mainly to satisfy their desire to please women. Take women out of their lives, and great wealth would be useless to most men. It is this inherent desire of man to please woman, which gives a woman the power to make or break a man" (Hill, 2011, p. 291).

To this analysis, I will now add my conclusions about physical attraction from the perspective of survivalism. In my last book, reproduction was ranked as a survival essential. However, it was not given as much weight as the other listed survival essentials. Actually, it was considered as a secondary physical immediate survival essential and not a primary one.

From *The Survival of the Richest*: "Next, we will look at our secondary physical immediate survival essentials. As these essentials may be too debatable for our current purposes, a ranking for them will not be provided. They may include but are not limited to beauty, companionship, fitness, good health, sanitation, and [reproductive] activity" (Criniti, 2016, p. 106).

Compare this list to what was listed as our primary physical immediate survival essentials (the most important requirements for our body for us to stay alive). These included, "Quality air and proper blood circulation, the thermal balance of the body, relief of immediate life-threatening bodily injuries, quality water, conservation of energy, a means to relieve bodily waste products, such as by defecation and urination, quality food, and quality sleep" (Criniti, 2016, p. 106).

Further, after my extensive research on survival, I added reproduction to the essentials list to avoid digressing from the scope of that book. From Many may consider reproduction "to be something they can't live without, which is why it was put on this list. However, the reason that sexual activity was not listed as a primary physical essential is because, contrary to common thinking, it is not necessary for the very immediate survival of an individual. It is, instead, necessary for the survival of humanity" (Criniti, 2016, p. 113).

It is also important to note that many of the survivors mentioned in this book have observed that reproduction was barely contemplated when the struggle included starvation; instead, food became the obsession. For example, as noted by Frankl of the people in the concentration camp, "Undernourishment, besides being the cause of the general preoccupation with food, probably also explains the fact that the sexual urge was generally absent" (Frankl, 2006, p. 32). "Our bodies need energy to make their systems run properly before they can spend it on reproductive matters" (Criniti, 2016, p. 113).

Based on my above research, you might conclude that I disagree with Napoleon Hill's analysis in this complex chapter. Actually, I agree with most of what he said. However, I wanted to put this subject in its proper context from a survival perspective. What I am adding is elevating the conversation to a macro level. When we understand the biological necessities of physical attraction, we can properly rank the energy we spend on this function.

Attraction energy certainly has a huge influence on what we do. If we can channel this energy properly, we can become a greater version of ourselves. Nevertheless, this can also be true if we channel our energies to obtaining other survival essentials. For example, how much energy do we waste in our lifetime obsessing over other survival essentials like food, clothing, and/or sleep?

Hunger, thirst, exhaustion, and other feelings related to our primary immediate survival essentials have been neglected in this argument of energy management for the purposes of genius elevation. These words can only be fully understood by those who have been deprived for an extensive period of time of any of those survival essentials listed above, for example, food. Simply, if you haven't eaten for a week, physical intimacy would be the last thing on your mind.

In short, if you can harness the energy targeted at all of your survival essentials, including intimacy, and redirect it towards your craft, you will decode the mystery of survival essentials transmutation. This is a more holistic approach to the subject of energy transmutation as the summation of all of your energy sources, targeted at obtaining biological necessities of your survival, can be unlocked and transmuted. You can now reach heights greater than Hill's conclusions could have imagined.

ANTHONY M. CRINITI IV

About Dr. Anthony M. Criniti IV: Dr. Anthony M. Criniti IV (aka "Dr. Finance®") is the world's leading financial scientist and survivalist. A fifth-generation native of Philadelphia, Dr. Criniti is a former finance professor at several universities, a former financial planner, an active investor in diverse marketplaces, an explorer, an international keynote speaker, and has traveled around the world studying various aspects of finance. He is an award-winning author of three #1 international Bestselling finance books: *The Necessity of Finance* (2013), *The Most Important Lessons in Economics and Finance* (2014), and *The Survival of the Richest* (2016). Dr. Criniti is also the host of the highly successful Dr. Finance® Live Podcast as well as one of the top hosts on Clubhouse. Dr. Criniti has started a grassroots movement that is changing the way that we think about economics and finance. Learn more about Doctor Finance at DrFinance.Info.

Author's Website: *www.DrFinance.info*

Book Series Website & Author's Bio: *www.The13StepsToRiches.com*

Barry Bevier

THE COST OF PROCRASTINATION

One definition of transmute is to change something completely, especially into something different and better. In *Think and Grow Rich*, The 10th Step to Riches is The Mystery of Sex Transmutation. Napoleon Hill describes redirecting sexual energy into other areas of life, such as creativity, productivity, and achievement. Sexual energy may be one of the most powerful forms of energy that a person can possess.

Many people view sexual energy as a positive force that can be channeled into creative endeavors, spiritual growth, or emotional connection with others. Human energy transmutation is to the idea that we can transform our mental, emotional, and physical energy into different forms, improving our overall well-being. It involves cultivating positive thoughts and emotions like love, gratitude, and compassion. By focusing our attention on these positive states, we can increase our overall energy levels and improve our mental and emotional health. Everything in the universe has a vibration and energy, whether positive or negative. Many thoughts and activities may produce negative energy. What if we could transmute the energy of a negative thought or behavior into something positive or creative?

The human brain is an incredibly complex organ, responsible for controlling all of our bodily functions, thoughts, emotions, and behaviors. Despite its relatively small size, about 2% of the body's weight, the brain uses about 20% of the body's total energy supply. This high level of energy consumption is necessary to support the brain's many functions, including maintaining the ability for neurons to communicate with each other, synthesizing neurotransmitters and other signaling molecules, and carrying out many processes involved in learning and memory.

Not surprisingly, different parts of the brain have different energy needs. The Prefrontal Cortex is the part of the brain responsible for planning, decision making, problem solving and creativity, mostly positive activities. It uses a disproportionate amount of energy compared to other parts of the brain. The Hippocampus, which is critical for learning and memory, also has high energy needs. The Amygdala is often referred to as the ancient or primitive brain. It also has high energy usage. Its role is to keep us safe from harm by quickly alerting us to potential dangers and triggering the body's fight or flight response. When it senses a threat, the Amygdala will immediately signal our body to prepare for action by increasing our heart rate and adrenaline production, so we can either flee or defend ourselves. It is a very active part of the brain and therefore uses a lot of energy to protect us from harm or avoid change.

Research suggests that negative thoughts may use more energy than positive thoughts. This is because negative thoughts activate the Amygdala, which can lead to stress hormones such as cortisol which requires more energy to produce. Conversely, positive thoughts tend to activate the Prefrontal Cortex. This activation leads to the release of dopamine, a neurotransmitter associated with pleasure and reward, which may require less energy to produce than cortisol.

I'm sure most of us have experienced days where we were extremely productive at problem-solving, being creative, or making decisions that left us joyful yet somewhat mentally fatigued. And I'm pretty sure there are days when we are mentally exhausted after worrying, attempting to be perfect or procrastinating on completing a task.

Take procrastination as an example, because it is a behavior I have battled much of my life, and I continue to work on it today. I've recently discussed with a mentor that perhaps procrastination is a choice, a concept I hadn't thought of before. We choose to put off large, complicated, and overwhelming tasks. Procrastination can be an energy-intensive process for the brain. When we procrastinate, our brains constantly battle our impulses to avoid difficult or unpleasant tasks and our goal to complete those tasks. This battle uses a lot of energy and cognitive resources, such as attention, memory, and self-control. As a result, procrastination can leave us feeling mentally drained and less able to focus on other tasks. In addition, research has shown that chronic procrastination can increase stress levels and anxiety, which further depletes our mental energy reserves.

My awareness that I was challenged with procrastination probably occurred when I went to college. There were often last-minute scrambles to complete projects or term papers that I knew were due from the beginning of the semester. There was last-minute cramming for exams. During my engineering career, there was more than just the occasional all-nighter at the office completing proposals or reports for clients. Nowadays, I may find myself packing at the last minute for a trip that has been planned for weeks. And working in the evening or on a weekend because I am behind schedule on something.

I remember one instance in high school when I was excited to showcase my freshly restored '57 Thunderbird at the local Fourth of July Parade. When I started the work, I had more than enough time to complete it well before the parade. However, I still ended up putting the finishing touches on it into the wee hours of the morning on the day of the parade. I made it, yet at what cost?

I have often attributed what is really procrastination to being too busy and not having enough time to get everything done. I tend to plan too much into a day or week, perhaps having unreasonable expectations of myself. When overwhelm sets in, my Amygdala goes into action, and I may freeze instead of tackling the big project in small chunks.

Procrastination can have significant costs in both terms of immediate consequences and long-term effects. One of the exercises we have done in my mastermind is to make a list of what procrastination has cost us in our lives. Here are my top five:

1. Stress - When we procrastinate, we often end up feeling stressed, overwhelmed, and anxious about the looming deadline or task. This negatively affects our mental and physical wellbeing which can lead to chronic health problems.

2. Wasted Time - Procrastination often results in wasted time. When we put things off, we usually spend more time than necessary on a task or project or rush to get things done at the last minute. And time is the only thing we can never get back in our lives. Once it's gone, it's gone.

3. Missed Opportunities - Procrastination can cause us to miss out on opportunities that had been available if we had acted earlier. Whether it's a job opportunity, a chance to network, or even a chance to learn something new, putting off things can result in missed opportunities.

4. Poor Quality of Work - When we wait until the last minute to complete a task, we end up shortcutting and producing less quality than we are capable of.

5. Damaged Reputation - Particularly in professional settings, repeatedly missing deadlines, failing to follow through on commitments, and poor quality work can damage our reputation. It can make others question our ability and competence. It can also damage personal relationships by being more stressed and spending time at work instead of with loved ones or friends.

So how can we transmute the negative energy of procrastination into a positive, creative thought or activity, or even just conserve it?

For years I attempted to fight procrastination by getting more organized, planning better, and committing to less. I made some progress, yet I still did not always get things done on time. After becoming aware of John

Ashraf and NeuroGym, I enrolled in his "Winning the Game of Procrastination" program. This was a game-changer for me. Since then, I have worked on maintaining better habits that helped me procrastinate less, get more done, have more energy to be productive and creative, and spend time with loved ones and friends. Here are five things that I have changed that have helped.

1. Eliminate or Reduce Distractions - Identify the things that distract us the most and do our best to eliminate or minimize them. For example, turning off our phones and social media while we're working.

2. Create a Schedule - Create a schedule or to-do list to help stay on track and make sure to prioritize the tasks and focus on the most important ones first.

3. Set Specific Goals - Start by setting clear and specific goals for what we would like to accomplish. Break them down into smaller manageable tasks and write them down. Put them in a calendar and stick to them.

4. Start with Smaller Tasks - Sometimes starting with a small, easy task can help build momentum and motivation to tackle the larger tasks.

5. Practice Self-Compassion - Acknowledge that most people procrastinate from time to time and that it's okay to make mistakes and have a setback. Treat ourselves with kindness and understanding. It is okay to work on it again tomorrow.

I have also started practicing meditation and tapping (EFT- Emotional Freedom Technique) every morning. This helps me relax, gain a higher vibration level, and create positive energy to start my day. Remember that changing a bad habit to a good one takes time and effort. We must be patient with ourselves and keep striving towards our goals.

BARRY BEVIER

About Barry Bevier: Barry Bevier is a proud father of two amazing daughters, who are pursuing their passions in psychology and architecture in Southern California where he lived, worked and raised a family for over 40 years. He recently moved to North Carolina to pursue the next adventure in his life's journey. Barry was raised on a family farm near Ann Arbor, Michigan. Growing up, he developed his faith in God, a strong work ethic, a love for nature, and a passion to help others. After completing his master's degree in civil engineering at the University of Michigan, he pursued a career in engineering, which eventually brought him to Southern California.

In 2000, he married the love of his life, Linda. They shared a beautiful life for ten years, until she succumbed to the effects of lupus and 20 years of treatment with prescription medications. Since then, Barry pivoted his career path into educating and helping others with their health and longevity. Barry has educated himself in alternative, natural modalities in wellness and became a Licensed Brain Health Expert through Amen Clinics. His primary focus and business is a new technology in stem cell supplementation that releases your own stem cells without invasive medical procedures.

Author's Website: *www.BRBevier.stemtech.com*

Book Series Website & Author's Bio: *www.The13StepsToRiches.com*

Bonnie Lierse

CREATIVE ENERGY ON STEROIDS

This is a wake-up topic based on Napoleon Hill's 13 principles! Not one you hear much about! We are always guided, by a higher source, on what to read or understand when we need it—especially in our awakening, after sixty-seven years, as I am living presently or proof!

Have you ever asked yourself who you are and what you have been programmed to believe about yourself?

I always ask myself now, "Who am I"? I recently went to a retreat at the Art of Living Retreat Center to awaken my spiritual senses. They knew that's where I was at in life. Now, I listen and allow subtle guidance. Guidance...I didn't understand in the past. I looked up the definition of "Transmutation," and here is what it said:

"Transmutation is channeling and redirecting your energy into a 'greater' purpose. It is one of the most powerful energies in existence. Our inner energy can be directed towards achieving and reaching our goals, manifesting the dreams we deeply desire, and experiencing a much deeper, and I mean much deeper, state of consciousness. It can be from your consciousness to your subconsciousness, to your super subconsciousness."

Even for me, that is intense. It's not a topic I thought I would or could discuss or write about.

Imagine losing your best friend and the love of your life, as I have been living this past year, as of November 23, 2021. We truly miss the intimacy with that true love; however, I'm learning on this journey about something called love. I did indeed forget about that! Always a work in progress!

I have been taught and am learning, as we speak, that energy can surface in creative energy and so much more.

I am reading many books by Rebecca Campbell. She is extremely spiritual on many levels! She states, "I found myself in love for the first time in my life—not with anyone, but with self." She was in the space of unconditional love! She also taught me the word "Shakti," which is defined as, "Spiritual life force that connects all of life." It means, "Unconditional love."

Rebecca Campbell also shares, "Your physical is holy. You are holy. May we unshackle ourselves from seeing ourselves as anything but this?"
I love this quote from her:

> *"Every woman is a Goddess, for she has the capacity to embody the divine feminine Shakti in full radiant force."*

We are always guided to what we need to understand and read when needed, as I am living proof and writing this chapter.

What all this is bringing out is: love! Not an easy place for anyone, including me! Many depend on others for that approval. I, included, was always seeking that approval. I lived it.

Now, I'm being guided in the transformation to comprehend self-love! Of course, you can still be in love with someone here on earth, even your soul flame, as I have had, but you can also feel love for yourself and redirect your energies to a more creative self. Writing is an example for me! This has been a powerful and surprising journey. Writing has become part of my creative energy, which I didn't know I had in me.

It is crucial that we are aware of our innate wisdom (intuition) and powerful, unconditional love!

I just came off a retreat for "Awakening My Senses," which was life changing. I am aware that we all have medium skills that need an awakening. We have great intuition, listening to our gut, and many Clair's not yet awakened. The incredible people in that room had mediumship gifts opening like a petal on a flower. You can awaken all your creative desires and energies without thinking about it!

"If you think and believe it, you can conceive it, or if you think it, so be it." Whatever is flowing in you, let it be organic! It will come naturally. You'll just know! You can manifest almost anything if you truly believe it hard enough! My journey has been an unexpected mystery! I know the creative juices are going to start pouring out! It will pour out so fast I won't be able to catch it!

With the loss of my love, it was and is also a bittersweet gain! However, I'm on a path that is surprising, not only to you and others but to myself! A dear friend of mine said this, "Time doesn't exist just on this linear plane. We have lived multiple lifetimes. I love that you're being taught from the other side. It's truly a beautiful thing when people are open to hearing and receiving. We miss important messages from the other side (guides, ancestors, etc.), so I think it's beautiful what you're doing." Thank you for sharing that! It's all true!

Through this unexpected path, my creative energy is starting to surface as we speak! So, I am definitely focused on THAT!

Did you know that as time on earth moves on, we can forget what we are designed to do or made for? For me, sixty-eight years later, it's beginning to resurface, whether it be my art, writing, spiritual awakening, and so much more! Sometimes, we must be creative just to communicate or sell ourselves! We always sell in some way, whether a product or service! Finding the right words to help someone evolve and believe in themselves is a huge undertaking and so worth it! Be creative!

For your information, my true love is the one, even now, bringing out the creative energy I had truly buried! Isn't that incredible?

What will bring out your creative energy? Do you have creative energy you want to surface? Sometimes, we don't know until it happens or surfaces!

What will explode your creative juices or energies? Everyone has them; we just forget under life's pressures! Think about when you were a baby or toddler—we didn't think twice about our creativity. We went with the flow! It seemed so natural. As we get older, sometimes we block the mindset! Don't be afraid to be spontaneous on your path! You'll truly love it! Seek your potential; it's there! Grab the coattails of anyone that will show you!

To bring this to a close or open a new door, take all your energies that you would put into hobbies and take those same extreme passions and intense energies and bring them out in your creative self! You will blow your mind with what can transpire from those energies! There is a deep creative self that wants to pour out of you! How exciting!

BONNIE LIERSE

About Bonnie Lierse: Bonnie Zaruches Lierse is extremely artistic and creative, with an entrepreneurial bent. Besides that, she is a seasoned agent with more than twenty years' experience in real estate in the New York/Long Island area. She relocated to Northern Virginia in 2012 and continued her real estate career there.

Another passion is creating leaders by working in business leadership development with *Leadership Team Development (LTD)*, and marketing products supplied by *Amway*. She was also a member of *The Screen Cartoonist Guild of Motion Pictures* for many years. Also, she did freelance for *Sesame Street* in New York City. In addition, she was a District Director for an interior accessory design company, as her own business.

Bonnie is blessed with five beautiful grandchildren and is very close with her children and family, some of whom are also in Virginia. Her missions are leadership, mentorship, paying it forward, and changing lives one at a time. Her motto is "You be the difference!"

Author's website: *www.amway.com/myshop/SplashFXEnterprises*

Book Series Website: *www.The13StepsToRiches.com*

Brian Schulman

FROM HERE TO THERE

Have you ever manifested anything? Saw it clearly in your mind, every detail, experienced the desire with every cell in your body, and had complete faith that it was going to happen as if it had already had? And then it did?

Transmutation.

Do you have a person to whom you gravitate because you know that you feel energized and alive whenever you are with them?

Transmutation.

Have you ever avoided doing something and found afterward that you were invigorated?

Transmutation.

Conversely, have you had the experience of being in a fantastic mood and then entering a room where everyone was complaining and left feeling drained?

And, yes, transmutation.

There are countless examples, but if you have ever experienced anything I have mentioned, you know the power of transmutation!

As a mastery coach working with C-Suite Executives, Sales Teams, and Entrepreneurs, I teach people how to be the hero of their own stories. How to make more money and not only gain revenue but have more time to do the things they love. Together, we change their business culture and, in doing so, transmute time and effort into revenue. As a result, everyone's satisfaction with, and success in, their roles is amplified.

Transmutation.

As the co-host of 2 global award-winning LIVE shows, I have had the privilege of turning people's day around, changing their outlook, positively impacting their mental health, inspiring them, and leaving them feeling better than before they came on and joined us!

A depressed 30-year marketing veteran and agency CEO gave me every reason why she COULD NOT show up LIVE on the show.

Her house was turned upside down because her kids were home from college due to Covid. Her hair was a mess. Her lighting was bad. Her bed was unmade. The list goes on. And realizing after I said...WHAT ELSE? The lightbulb went off for her—just as I said it - we are ALL going through the same experience—TOGETHER.

Using Napoleon Hill's third step to riches, Auto-Suggestion, I was able to help her see that the playing field was leveled for EVERYONE. And THAT is relatable.

She showed up at her desk, baseball cap backward, which was so not her style, bed behind her, and said with a smile on her face, "...'Welcome to Wendy's Frat House.'"

She showed up every week for a year, then forward to be on the show.

Why? She said it made her FEEL better.

Transmutation.

Transmutation, as stated by Napoleon Hill in his (award-winning) book *"Think and Grow Rich,"* is "The changing, or transferring of one element, or form of energy, into another."

Have you ever heard of the expression your network is your net worth? How your network your pipeline, life source, and conduit to success? Well, HOW you build your network is as important as BUILDING a network. Time is your most valuable commodity. Building relationships is key to success in anything. When I meet with people, I ask them what it is that you love. What is it that lights you up? What brings you to life? I ask this because you can return to the things you love more quickly by transmuting your time and efforts into profit while gaining more time.

Take, for example, an experienced Voice Your Vibe's Chief Engagement Officer, Nancy Debra Barrows, recently had.

As a conversation took place between her and a member of the audience who had just heard her Keynote Address at a conference, I observed. He was speaking about his best friend who has cancer and whom he wanted to help. He expressed that he didn't know how to ask the question without feeling like he was being offensive or having it be awkward. He also felt that because it was his best friend, he should already know what he needed and not have to ask.

As Nancy brought up points and questions, his persistence that there was no way he could be comfortable asking required her to use her imagination. She asked if he would feel uncomfortable if someone asked him what he needed, and he said, "Yes." Surprisingly, to most people in the room, she told him to get over himself and gracefully pointed out how he was making the situation more about himself than his best friend —with those words, Nancy was able to shift his perspective, which helped him feel less uncomfortable. Using her specialized knowledge in Social Cognition, she was able to speak his language so that her message was delivered in a way he could hear.

Together, they found words comfortable for him to say to his friend. Less than 24 hours later, he texted her to share that he had stepped out of his comfort zone and used the tools she had offered. He told her how amazing the conversation was, how much he had learned, how he now knew what his best friend needed in support, and that it was nothing he ever would have guessed. He was so happy that he had asked and would not have, had they not talked.

A 15-minute conversation led to the transmutation of energy from resistance to flow.

A 15-minute conversation led to the transmutation of energy from hesitation to confidence.

A 15-minute conversation led to the transmutation of energy from doubt to knowing.

A 15-minute conversation led to a transmutation of energy that shifted back to his true intention, which was to help his best friend.

His time with Nancy and the results they yielded led to him actively finding clients for Nancy that he knew she could help after this transmutation experience.

These moments of converting clients into advocates are one of the best ways to transmute your time and energy to revenue and opportunities.

15 minutes.

15 minutes and he was referring clients to Nancy.

15 minutes and he was calling the organizer of a national conference and got Nancy a spot as a speaker at one of the largest conferences in the podcasting industry.

15 minutes and he was introducing Nancy to influential people who are now setting up events with sponsors to spotlight her, her work, Voice Your Vibe, our two global award-winning live shows, our Master Classes, and Mastermind.

My investment in Nancy and my decision to help her with the organized planning to build her business by inviting her to be Co-host to the shows and bringing her on board as the Chief Engagement Officer at Voice Your Vibe led her to invest time in someone else. But, in doing so, she brought that opportunity back to me. So, my original investment has been transmuted to revenue, opportunities and deeper networking without requiring any more of my time.

That transmutation of feelings and energy is a powerful conduit to success.

As Maya Angelou says, "People might forget would you say, but they will never forget how you make them feel."

Meeting a first-time guest and his special-needs son on one of our two global award-winning LIVE shows, an investment of 10 minutes, which left us all feeling like a million dollars, was transmuted into a business that is converting the current mindset of vanity metrics to reality metrics, where more transmutation can take place.

The time you spend building your network, your tribe, and your community transmutes to opportunities and revenue you never thought possible.

BRIAN SCHULMAN

About Brian Schulman: Named 'The King of Community on LinkedIn' by Forbes and known as 'The Godfather and Pioneer of LinkedIn Video' and one of the world's premiere live streaming & video marketing experts, Brian Schulman is a 9X #1 Bestselling Author (and 5X #1 International Bestselling Author) and internationally renowned Keynote Speaker, whose expertise, insights, and two Global Award-Winning LinkedIn LIVE Shows have been featured on NASDAQ, Forbes, Thrive Global, Bloomberg, Yahoo Finance, CBS, NBC, FOX, Viacom, Roku TV, Amazon Fire, PODTV, The CW, and hundreds of shows and podcasts, reaching millions worldwide.

Brian brings his twenty-plus years of experience, wealth of knowledge, and proven leadership expertise to C-Suite Executives and Entrepreneurs globally as an advisor and mentor through Voice Your Vibe's groundbreaking masterminds and heart-centered leadership programs. Brian has been named a 6X LinkedIn Top Voice, LinkedIn Video Creator of the Year, 3X Top 50 Most Impactful People of LinkedIn, 4X Rising Star & Influencer to Watch on LinkedIn and 2X LinkedIn Global Leader of The Year, out of one billion business professionals on LinkedIn. Brian is also the Executive Producer, Creator and Cohost of VoiceYourVibe LIVE, which includes two global award-winning weekly LinkedIn LIVE shows broadcast in 120+ countries that have aired for over five years and 500+ consecutive episodes—and were named "Best LIVE Festive Show of The Year" at the IBM TV Awards.

Author's Website: *www.VoiceYourVibe.com*

Book Series Website & Author's Bio: *www.The13StepsToRiches.com*

Candace & David Rose

TRANSMUTE TRANSFORMATION

*"The meaning of the word
'transmute' is, in simple language,
'the changing, or transferring of
one element, or form of energy,
into another.'"*
~ Napoleon Hill

CANDACE & DAVID ROSE

About Candace and David Rose: Candace and David are #1 Bestselling Authors in the book series *The 13 Steps to Riches*. They grew up together and currently live in Alvarado, Texas, with their six children, two chickens, one dog, four cats, and a rabbit. They both are veterans of the US Army. David served as a mechanic, and Candace as a Legal NCO.

David is currently a Product Release Specialist, delivering Liquid Oxygen and Nitrogen to various manufacturing plants and hospitals throughout Texas. Candace specializes in helping people organize their space, both physically and mentally—with the ultimate goal to help you change your box and find more joy in your life.

Author's Website: *www.ChangeYourBox.com*

Book Series Website & Author's Bio: *www.The13StepsToRiches.com*

Corey Poirier

TRANSMUTATION AND MY ADMISSION

This was the chapter in this series that I had the hardest part in starting and writing.

Interestingly enough, it wasn't until I interviewed John Gray (*Men are from Mars*) that everything came together for me to dive in.
During our conversation, John talked about life force and the power of redirecting our transmutative energy.

He spoke about how he has more energy now in his 70s than many people his age. He even said the advice he could give his younger self if he could step into a time machine and go back he would tell himself to stop using all of his life force on a daily basis.

I have a person in my network whose core focus these days is talking to people, mostly men, about redirecting their energy and the power of life force and the infinite intelligence you can acquire when you are willing to redirect your transmutative energy.

I must admit this one stumped me for a long time when I read the book.

It's almost like if you're eating all organic food, you are more likely to have to explain why you choose this diet over eating processed food than if you just had a "normal" diet, especially in years past. You also have to explain more that you are choosing to not use your life force than you do if you are using it daily.

Admittedly it was also hard for me to grasp the idea of redirecting my energy.

I have never felt that I could truly feel my energy or the energy of others, and so trying to redirect something I can't feel—it seems to be foreign and abstract.

That said, I am currently trying this idea of redirecting my transmutative energy, and I have to say I already feel a bit more clearly.

Whether it's a placebo thing or I'm really experiencing a difference, I guess I need more time to determine that. Still, I'm all for anything that can increase my goal-achieving ability and overall energy.

I think the other thing that makes this appealing to me is that I have never liked the idea of giving up control to anyone else or urges.

I also like the idea of increasing the vibrations of my thought.

I especially considered the fact that this energy is among the main stimuli of the mind, and here I had been depleting my life force unknowingly.

Here I am, just starting my journey of redirecting my life force, not knowing what the result will be but knowing it could mean better health and a clearer mind.

While in the other chapters I have contributed, I was able to share facts, teachings, lessons, and my experience with the content of that section; in this case, instead, it sees me trying something new.

So, this chapter submission is simply my admission that I'm still learning. This is yet another example of *Think and Grow Rich* giving back to me years after my initial reading.

I do know the promises of energy transmutation, and I know I want to realize those promises.

In this chapter, though, I simply wanted to make a case for being vulnerable and realizing we should never start learning and growing.

Perhaps in the future, I'll be able to report my full experience with building my life force. Until then, thank you for reading, and here's to your greater success.

Corey's Contact Info:

Facebook: *www.facebook.com/corey.poirier.1*

Linkedin: *www.linkedin.com/in/speakercoreypoirier*

Instagram: *www.instagram.com/thatspeakerguy*

Email: *blutalksbrand@gmail.com*

COREY POIRIER

About Corey Poirer: Corey Poirier is a multiple-time TEDx Speaker. He is also the host of the top-rated *Let's Do Influencing* Radio Show, founder of the growing bLU Talks brand, and has been featured in multiple television specials. He is also a Barnes and Noble, Amazon, Apple Books, and Kobo Bestselling Author, Award-Winning Author, and the co-author of the *Wall Street Journal / USA Today* Bestseller, *Quitless*. A columnist with *Entrepreneur* and *Forbes* magazines, he has been featured in/on various mediums. He is one of the few leaders featured twice on the popular *Entrepreneur on Fire* show. He has also interviewed over 6,500 of the world's top leaders. He has spoken on-site at Harvard, Columbia University, and more recently to Microsoft team leaders and at Kyle Wilson's Inner Circle retreat, featuring everyone from Brian Tracy to Mark Victor Hansen to Phil Collen (Def Leppard).

Also appearing on the popular Evan Carmichael YouTube Channel, he is a New Media Summit Icon of Influence, was recently listed as the #5 Influencer in Entrepreneurship by Thinkers 360 and listed on the 2021 Brainz CREA Global Awards as an honoree. He is a Humanitarian Hero Award Nominee, Entrepreneur of the Year Nominee, Champion Award (Business from The Heart) nominee, and, to demonstrate his versatility, a Rock Recording of the Year Nominee who has performed stand-up comedy more than 700 times, including an appearance at the famed Second City.

Author's Website: *www.ThatSpeakerGuy.com*

Book Series Website & Author's Bio: *www.The13StepsToRiches.com*

Deb Scott

CHANNEL THE UNKNOWN

"People who are driven by this desire—in a positive, constructive sense—can 'channel' it to develop keenness of imagination, courage, willpower, persistence, and creative ability that are all but unknown at other times."
~ Napoleon Hill

DEB SCOTT

About Deb Scott: Deb Scott, BA, CPC, and Realtor, was a high honors biology major at Regis College in Weston, Massachusetts, and spent over two decades as an award-winning cardio-thoracic sales specialist in the New England area. She is a Bestselling Author of *The Sky is Green & The Grass is Blue: Turning Your Upside Down World Right Side Up*. She is an award-winning podcaster of *The Best People We Know Show*. Following in her family's footsteps, she is a third-generation Realtor in Venice, Florida. As a certified life coach, Deb speaks and teaches on how to turn bad situations into positive, successful results. As a top sales specialist, she enjoys teaching people "sales without selling," believing that integrity, good communication, and respect are the winning equation to all outstanding success and happiness in life.

Author's Website: *www.DebScott.com*

Book Series Website & Author's Bio: *www.The13StepsToRiches.com*

Dori Ray

THE MOTIVATING FORCE

"When 'harnessed' and 'redirected' constructively, this motivating force maintains all of its attributes of keenness of imagination, courage, and so forth, which may be used as powerful creative forces in literature, art, or in any other profession, calling, or undertaking—including, of course, the accumulation of riches."
~ Napoleon Hill

DORI RAY

About Dori Ray: Dori "On Purpose" Ray is a native Philadelphian. As a businesswoman, her mission is to help people transform their minds, bodies, and bank accounts!

Dori was educated in the Philadelphia Public School System. She graduated from the Philadelphia High School for Girls in 1982 and Howard University School of Business in 1986 with a BBA in Marketing. Dori is a Delta Sigma Pi Business Fraternity and Delta Sigma Theta Sorority, Inc. member.

Dori leads teams around the world. She is a sought-after Speaker and Trainer within her industry and beyond. She is an experienced Re-Entry Coach who has helped hundreds of Returning Citizens get back on track after incarceration.

Having suffered from depression for 20 years, she always reaches back to share her story and help break the cycle of silence. Her audience loves her authenticity! Book Dori for speaking engagements with her information below.

Author's Website: *www.linktr.ee/DoriOnPurpose*

Book Series Website & Author's Bio: *www.The13StepsToRiches.com*

Elaine Sugimura

BLOSSOMING FROM SURVIVING TO THRIVING

So much of my history is centered around the health challenges I faced as a young woman, wife, and mother. I was in the second half of my roaring 20s and felt so blessed with all I had achieved thus far in life. I married the man of my dreams, gave birth to two healthy handsome boys, and my business career was on the move—upward! Keeping my head down and constantly striving to be the best at all the things I touched or was responsible for was how I managed LIFE. If I received the recognition and compensation, nothing could stop my desire to reach past the glass ceiling in Corporate America. Then one day, I felt the bright lights turn off.

My first bout with breast cancer was at the age of 29. The Game of Life was just at its starting point, and there was nothing but greatness happening all around me. I did not have time for this illness, nor was I willing to allow it to derail my plans. The only way through was to BE the SURVIVOR I was willing to BE. I did not allow the illness to take over my mind, body, or spirit. I continued to live my life the way I managed the game of life—powerfully: with the aliveness I felt deep down from my toes to the top of my head and with courage, love, joy, and inspiration.

If my life's strategy was to stay intact, I knew causing and creating the result I wanted was paramount at all costs. The physical being was less important that the mindful being. I knew this was key to surviving this deadly disease. I was ready to tackle cancer head-on and was unwavering regarding treatment, placing myself first over all others. And, all the while knowing that I may lose what I loved most in life: my family.

The risk I was willing to take was shutting everyone out of my life so that I could concentrate on fighting this uphill battle. I had no room to worry about the healthy while dealing with possibly dying from this deadly disease. I placed the energy of surviving into healing and never asked the question of why *me*? I successfully landed in remission, and the Game of Life continued.

My second bout with breast cancer chose to show up when I was 41 years old. I had reached the pinnacle of my fashion executive career; the boys were now in college and high school, and life was exciting. For a moment, I felt like I had blossomed from surviving to thriving. Of course, this was another setback as this was not a reoccurrence: it was a newly diagnosed breast cancer, and it was aggressive.

There is no time to tell the entire story, so I can share that the game I was playing was in a time-out, and I got to reassess where I stood at that moment. I gave so much of myself the first round of treatment and was unclear on how to proceed with this diagnosis. Again, with my head held up high, I leaned in, one foot in front of the other; I chose to move forward with the fierceness a white tigress would canvas her land.

I chose the path of a mastectomy (for the second time) with full reconstruction. I had the DIEP procedure, which essentially means I used my own skin and fat to rebuild both breasts. My left breast would need a full reconstruction as I had a modified radical mastectomy with my first bout. My doctor suggested a lumpectomy by removing all the breast tissue in my right breast. At the time, only two doctors in the U.S. performed the DIEP surgery. The surgery would take eighteen hours in total, and I remained under anesthesia the entire time. My gas tank was running on empty, and I knew that surviving this deadly disease required me to find the energy to fill my gas tank back up to full.

Once again, I fought and endured the eighteen-hour surgery and multiple tubes and drains to feel whole again and hear that the surgery was a success. The Game of Life would continue, and, once again, I was labeled a SURVIVOR squared.

So where does this deep seeded energy come from? What prompted me to ignore the diagnosis and treat it like any other health issue? It is the exact same energy that allowed me to achieve all that I have thus far in my life. There was never a doubt in my mind that I would overcome either of the breast cancer diagnoses. Never looking back, always in the present, my "LIFE IS NOW" mantra rang true to anything else being shared or said to me.

Looking forward to the future and choosing goals that would allow me to achieve the best that life had to offer me. I simply wanted to see my two sons graduate from high school, and as each year passed, the goals were further out. Graduation from college, getting married, having grandchildren. All dreams at the beginning, and through this positive energy that rang through each cell of my body, I knew I had become a THRIVER in my life. No longer blossoming as a survivor, I had now moved towards blossoming as a thriver. So, let's explore what it takes to stay in that energy constantly, in body, mind, and spirit.

Navigating the full landscape of my life required focus, stamina, courage, and showing up in my full vulnerability and authenticity. There was never a time I viewed my glass as half empty. I recognize today, as I look in the rear-view mirror, I chose to view my life as a glass that was always half full or more. It never felt right to just merely survive the day-to-day. As the speed bumps appeared, I knew with full clarity that every path I chose would lead me to either achieving what I set out to accomplish or down a path of possible destruction.

With both eyes wide open, I chose to stay in the positive energy that got me through the most difficult times of my life. You see, when you are faced with the possibility of death, the wake-up call that comes next is LIFE is NOW, so start living it. Good, bad, right, or wrong with no blame, shame, fault, or guilt, I was choosing to live my life fully and show up in the same energy that allowed me to WIN. I chose to transmute that positive energy as I roamed this place we call earth. With every fiber of my body, I chose to become a thriver both personally and professionally.

As I continue to seek higher levels of thriver-ship, I am exploring new ways of sharing my huge vision that encompasses how we can inspire others to recognize the possibility of blossoming from surviving to thriving and beyond. I have been contemplating for years what I could cause and create where individuals and groups of people would come together and create what I would call the Land of Thrive. It would be full of positive energy flow as only those who speak from their heart, not their head, have achieved the ultimate metric: creating a life of well-being, wisdom, and absolute wonder.

I have spent a great deal of time over my 60 years on this planet, and I am on a mission to inspire others to take hold of this powerful vision and own it as their own. Only then will I truly know that transmitting this high energy frequency to others is when the survivor has blossomed into the thriver within. Looking back from the start of it all to where I am today, transmuting all this positive energy and that stick-to-itiveness is why I am here today.

I remember vividly the two times I allowed tears to fall when I heard the words breast cancer. At that moment, I chose to wipe away those tears. I dug deep into my mind, body, and spiritual being to create the energy needed to be a survivor. I drew upon every success I experienced along this life's path and chose to play on a championship team, as winning was the only option to stay alive.

What I would love for each of you to take away from this game of life is to remember the following: Don't just EXIST. LIVE your LIFE. Roam the Planet, EXPLORE, and BE ADVENTUROUS. BE A THRIVER, challenge yourself, challenge authority, and EVOLVE into the human you want and get to BE. Navigate, along with me, to the LAND of THRIVE. I know many of you are already here, but for those who are not, we are waiting for YOU. This is what I call "Inspired Living: Blossoming from Surviving to Thriving & Beyond." I leave you with this quote:

"The question is not how to survive but how to thrive with passion, compassion, humor & style."
~ Maya Angelou

ELAINE SUGIMURA

About Elaine R. Sugimura: Elaine is an accomplished CEO turned Business Consultant / Life Strategist who has a passion to create Leaders amongst Leaders. With over 35+ years in the fashion and food and beverage industry, she has a passion to not only lead but support those who are seeking to reinvent who they are, no matter where they are in life. She is a two-time breast cancer survivor and she knows a thing or two about surviving to thriving. Fun fact: she is an adrenaline junkie —the higher, the faster, the better. Her love for adventure has led her to travel to many parts of the world by plane, train and automobile.

She and her husband, Hiro, share their home in Northern California. They have raised two extraordinary sons, Bryce and Cole, and have added two beautiful daughters-in-law, Erica and Giselle, to their growing family. Her legacy is to share what is possible when we open ourselves up to the issues that hold us back. Her Life's mission is to move those who are just surviving into Thrivers!

Author's Website: *www.ElaineRSugimura.com*

Book Series Website & Author's Bio: *www.The13StepstoRiches.com*

Elizabeth Anne Walker

GESTATION

They say we are created in our grandmother's womb. A dark secret space in which all human creation occurs, a portal between spirit and tangible humanity, from the ether to reality. A cavernous space we all exit, yet the smallest tunnel is utilized to enter. A space where conditions are perilous, yet the rewards are life and vitality!

Energy to create transmutation is often nothing more than a behavioral response. Sometimes the energy behind this is somewhat an animalistic act. When directed towards desire alone, it can create a human life or ecstatic pleasure. When harnessed, held, and utilized for forms of creation, it can change the world! Few have the discipline or drive to achieve this.

Here I am reminded of Andrew Lloyd Weber's song from *Phantom of the Opera, Music of the night*, and the line, "Darkness stirs and wakes imagination." I ponder if this is how new creation occurs. The darkness of the womb stirs and imagining a new life is created. And I wonder how many have considered the need for darkness to be stirred first? Stirring to an action.

So, the action awakens the imagination, and the energy once put into the pursuit of desire is harnessed and utilized to imagine something of greatness. The passionate creative energies are all the same when releasing a great idea, product, or service into the world. And have you ever considered that?

Every single great idea, product, or service went through a period of gestation. Some are as short as that of a gnat, and some longer than that of an elephant. They all started in the darkness, the darkness was awoken through action, and then the journey begins. Along the way, the idea is fertilized, some independently like a butterfly and some through the contribution of others.

This is when the idea begins to become a reality, forming slowly at first until it takes on a momentum of growth on its own and then develops into something others start to recognize. It grows and grows and then becomes global in nature, where everyone knows about it.

And here is the question of what came first, the chicken or the egg? Did the idea come first, or the discipline to hold the energy and focus on the unknown to create the idea. And where did the energy come from? So many questions with few solid answers yet many postulations.
So, I will share my thoughts.

An idea comes in from the ether, and those ready and willing have early access to the idea. They align with their goals, have the energetic capacity, and know how to make decisions. Then there are those not ready, not even standing on the edge of anticipation. They're focused on all the wrong things, in all the wrong places, at all the wrong times, for them.

Knowing this led me to a search for the genesis of transmutation. Where does it start exactly? How can we transmute more easily through knowledge of the exact beginning point? To start, we must first make sense of what transmutation is.

So, transmutation is to have successive alteration and change. This implies that one type of change is never enough and that the change must be ongoing and successive. Therefore, to achieve transmutation, the energetics required are those of continuance. And the proof of this lies in those that are successful who say they are continually changing. Tony Robbins defines this as CANI (continuous and never-ending improvement). The concept is that success only eludes those that stop. However, knowing that transmutation is an ongoing journey doesn't show us how to get started.

We know that energy is required to start and keep going, yet no one tells us where this initially comes from. So, how do we start the process? This is the fun part! The energy is already within us! There is no need to generate it at all. It's merely about focusing it in the right direction!

We need to direct energy away from what we are currently focusing on and don't want and move it towards what we want! Okay, okay! I'll break it down more....

We have energy that we already use for multiple things: eating, resting, happiness, and sadness, for example. Our negative energy is often focused on what we don't want. For example, I don't want pain as opposed to feeling healthy and well. So, in a nutshell, when we focus on what we want and take action to move to what we want, we can change the course of our life!

And as with all things, there is a gestation period, a darkness if you will, while we learn to be the person we want to be, to do the things we want to do, to put us in a place where we can focus on what we want.

This implies that it's not a ride in the park. It will require effort, determination, and skill. The focus will need to be attentive every day, in every moment!

The alchemy of moving from what you don't want to what you do want will create incredible results that can be life-changing!

So here are the steps:

1. Turn your focus to what you want: When you start out, you will first consider the thing you don't want and then turn that picture into what you do want.

2. Visualize what you want daily: Practicing creating in your mind the vision of what you want will, over time, teach your unconscious mind a new pattern where instead of seeing a threat, it sees a reward.

3. Act as if: Be the person with the attitude to get the desired result. You won't see a millionaire hanging out watching TV in the middle of the day!

4. Honor the Law of Gestation: Things take time—allow yourself time to acknowledge all you're becoming and all you're letting go of in your life as you transmute this energy.

5. Respect the darkness: That's where all the best things are created. It may feel dark emotionally, physically, and financially for a time, but creation is occurring here. You are on track.

6. Keep Going: The fastest way to fail is to give up.

7. Refocus: Ensure what you want is still the same, create the vision, and hold on.

8. Hold strong to the faith you have transmuted before: Keep going and going and going!

At any point, if you get lost or feel your energy dropping, just start again. Transmutation is the energy behind any change: the transformation of one thing into another, the energetic shift towards as opposed to away from. Transmutation is the ability to be patient and keep going, to allow time for the physical, chemical, spiritual, emotional, gestational, generational, and mental aspects to align to create the darkness of where all creation begins. Then it's the effort to keep your eyes on the prize as it comes to fruition, to continue to call forth the energy from within to pull it from the depths of who you are, to support that creation.

You have done this before in your mother's womb when you were in darkness and focused on forming, differentiating, and growing. Transmutation is within you—you just have to remember you have that power. Much love as you traverse this journey into the unknown you've known all along.

ELIZABETH ANNE WALKER

About Elizabeth Walker: Elizabeth is Australia's leading Female Integrated NLP Trainer, an international speaker with Real Success, and the host of Success Resources's (Australia's largest and most successful events promoter, including speakers such as Tony Robbins and Sir Richard Branson) inaugural Australian Women's Program "The Seed." Elizabeth has guided many people to achieve complete personal breakthroughs and phenomenal personal and business growth. With over 25 years of experience transforming the lives of hundreds of thousands of people, Elizabeth's goal is to assist leaders to create the reality they choose to live, impacting millions on a global scale.

A thought leader who has worked alongside people like Gary Vaynerchuck, Kerwin Rae, Jeffery Slayter, and Kate Gray, Elizabeth has an outstanding method of delivering heart with business. As a former lecturer in medicine at the University of Sydney and lecturer in nursing at Western Sydney University, Elizabeth was instrumental in the research and development of the stillbirth and neonatal death pathways, ensuring each family in Australia went home knowing what happened to their child, and felt understood, heard, and seen.

A former Australian Champion in Trampolining and Australian Dance sport, Elizabeth has always been passionate about the mindset and skills required to create the results you are seeking.

Author's Website: *www.ElizabethAnneWalker.com*

Book Series Website & Author's Bio: *www.The13StepsToRiches.com*

Erin Ley

CONTROL THY ENERGY

In the classic book, *Think and Grow Rich,* Napoleon Hill brilliantly states, "The meaning of the word "transmute" is in simple language: 'the changing, or transferring of one element, or form of energy, into another."

As a Life Coach and Business Strategist, for thirty years I've been helping my clients transmute negative energy and transform it into greatly expanded energy focused on making your dreams your reality. A few examples of how I did this in my own life are as follows:

- Cancer diagnoses at age 25

- Three miscarriages in my 30's

- Divorce at age 47

Those life-defining moments for me each could have not just brought me to my knees as they did; they could have kept me there. However, I learned with the cancer diagnosis in 1991 that we are way more than just our physical bodies. We have way more control over our lives than most people know. We are, quite literally, the creators of our own life every second of every day.

First, the cancer diagnosis made me realize that my inner world was much more than I learned in 5th-grade science. I was not just made up of organs, bones, blood flow, and so on. I also had an energy system and a spiritual side to me inside that, as a child, was not spoken about in my home growing up, in school, and not even at Sunday mass. I spent my whole life looking to the outer world for validation for everything—until I had the greatest breakthrough of my life in May of 1991 when I was diagnosed with non-Hodgkin's lymphoblastic lymphoma, a rare pediatric form of cancer with a two-and-a-half-year protocol.

The doctors said if the chemotherapy didn't work as fast as the tumor was growing, I'd be dead in a month. I had thirty days to figure it out. And I did. From the hospital bed, I read tons of personal and professional development books and listened to cassette tapes as well. I craved learning more and more. This was when I learned about my whole inner world, what I could do for myself in curing myself of cancer, and transmuting my negative energy of fear, chaos, and confusion into faith, optimism, and love. I began to love myself and my connection with God more than I ever knew possible. I wrote down a crystal-clear vision for my life, goals that were beyond my wildest dreams because I had nothing to lose. I began to bring those goals to fruition at record speed. I kept living every time the doctors said I'd die, and I went on to have three healthy children that the doctors swore would never happen.

I intentionally transmuted the pain I was feeling physically, emotionally, mentally, intellectually, and spiritually into love and well-being, focused on excellent health and solution rather than the pain. I directed all of that harnessed energy toward my dreams and created a beautiful life for myself. The doctors at Memorial Sloan-Kettering Cancer Center started having their patients call me at home, and that's how I started life coaching in the 1990s. I did it for free for years because I was on fire to empower cancer patients with what I learned. The doctors could not explain it. They explained to me that I should be doing it for a living because the patients were coming to the hospital with a new outlook on life, tolerating the chemotherapy and radiation a lot better. I taught them how to transmute their energy, and everything changed for them.

In 1999, after having my first son, Brendan, on December 13, 1997, I experienced a miscarriage. It was devastating. I was twelve weeks, had just gotten through the first trimester, told friends and family the great news, and then during a routine visit, there was no heartbeat. The doctor and the staff had to take me through the private hallways I had no idea existed to walk me out to my car, where my husband sat waiting. I was screaming and crying that the tech had done the sonogram wrong, that everyone was wrong, and that my baby did not die. I was in shock and couldn't speak to anyone for three months. I went on to find out that I had to wait two years to try again. Two years later, I experienced two more miscarriages, leaving me questioning my faith in God. I was furious with Him. One day, sitting on my bed, I realized that I had to begin to transmute the all-encompassing pain. I had to do what I did with the cancer and create a vision for what I wanted, harness the negative energy, transmute it, and direct the transmuted energy in the direction of my dreams.

As a Roman Catholic who was furious with God, I started by going to confession. Everyone in line in the church waiting for their turn had to have felt my fury. Finally, I was able to go into the confessional booth. Bless me, Father, for I have sinned; it's been about ten years since my last confession. I'm furious with God, and that's a problem. Please help me with this!

To this day, I don't remember what the priest said, but it was comforting and reassuring. I sat in one of the pews in the church, said my penance, and cried all the way home in my car—the most cathartic cry. Finally, I felt free of the burden. I went home and reviewed my vision statement with a new positive mental attitude coupled with a restored faith that was strengthened once again: I soon found out that I was pregnant! Danny was born on December 19, 2001. Four months after Danny was born, I conceived my daughter, Maggie, and she was born on April 18, 2003.

Miracles come in threes, and I credit transmutation and my massive faith in God for these incredible blessings.

My ex-husband and I were together for twenty-two years. Once again, I was shocked and thrown back on my heels when he decided he preferred a bar stool over family and home. After he left, I was shocked and confused. It was so similar to the cancer diagnosis whereby my identity came into question, my future was thrown in the air, and it all happened so suddenly. The rage I felt is indescribable. It was unhealthy. So many negative things kept happening: The hot water heater flooded my basement; a car hit my car from behind. I began to understand very quickly that I had to change my thoughts rapidly and transmute my negative energy into expanded positive energy to begin attracting the right people, places, and things that would bring me the ultimate destiny I desired.

I updated my vision statement, writing out, pen to paper, exactly what I wanted to create for myself personally and professionally. I've been able to check off every one of the goals. I've never been happier, healthier, and wealthier than I am these days. I grew my coaching practice to six figures in a year and a half and with the help of mentors, the Habitude Warrior Mastermind, the marketing company I hired, and the partnership I formed with another company helping business owners experience rapid revenue results. I'm working on scaling this year to seven figures.

This principle, transmutation, is so powerful. When you learn how to do this, and you begin to master transmuting the negative energy into an energy that can bring about miracles in your life, then you're unstoppable. The world becomes a playground where you'll have fun creating things at will. Guard your thoughts and feelings carefully. This is where our energy is given power. Energy cannot be created or destroyed. It's eternal. The power we want to give must be positive to create a great life for ourselves. If you feed the negative energy and do not transmute it, it will only lead to a life of suffering. You have control over all of this.

I learned this in 1991 and have been sharing this knowledge and wisdom ever since. I love watching my coaching clients transform in magnificent ways. When you can go from feeling overwhelmed and having self-doubt to becoming focused, fearless, and excited about life, you are living life on your terms. You will be in the driver's seat of your own life. When life is driving you, it is bumpy, with unexpected twists and turns that cause fear. You now have direction on how to create the best life for yourself.

Feel free to contact me if you would like a complimentary coaching consultation where we can discuss what might be holding you back from living your best life and what you can do to get your life on track.

Control thy energy! And always remember to live onward and upward!

ERIN LEY

About Erin Ley: As Founder and CEO of Onward Productions, Inc., Erin Ley has spent the last 30 years as an Author, Professional Speaker, Personal and Professional Empowerment and Success Coach predominantly around mindset, vision and decision. Founder of many influential summits, including "Life On Track," Erin is also the host of the upcoming online streaming T.V. show, "Life On Track with Erin Ley," which is all about helping you get into the driver's seat of your own life.

They call Erin "The Miracle Maker!" As a cancer survivor at age 25, single mom of 3 at age 47, successful Entrepreneur at age 50, Erin has shown thousands upon thousands across the globe how to become victorious by being focused, fearless, and excited about life and your future! Erin says, "Celebrate life and you'll have a life worth celebrating!"

To see more about Erin and the release of her 4th book, *WorkLuv: A Love Story*, along with her "Life On Track" Course & Coaching Programs, please visit her website.

Author's Website: *www.ErinLey.com*

Book Series Website & Author's Bio: *www.The13StepsToRiches.com*

Fatima Hurd

TRANSMUTING ENERGY: CONFIDENT EXPRESSION

"Transmute" is, in simple language, "the changing or transferring of one element, or form of energy, into another."
~ Napoleon Hill

Napoleon Hill explains how those who have mastered transmutative energy through a different form of expression are truly genius.

However, in the modern-day, we have been given access to tools that help us gain that same state of mind through other forms of expression. For example, Napoleon Hill explains that "intimate personal desire is one of the most powerful energies of human desire; when driven by this desire, people develop keenness of imagination, courage, willpower, persistence, and creative ability unknown to man at other times."

Another form of expression that can render similar results is confidence. Being confident means feeling or showing confidence in oneself and being self-assured, which aligns with Napoleon Hill's explanation of transmutative emotion, containing the secret of creative ability, defined as **the ability to present oneself without inhibitions, limitations, or anxiety freely**. It also relates to one's preparedness to function at the maximum level of competence, free from self-consciousness.

Dr. Wayne Dyer said it best: "A man's strongest desire is to be free in mind. Our soul's biggest desire is to be free to expand and reach out and embrace the infinite. The idea of the soul is infinity. Our soul hates being restricted and limited."

I have given this a lot of thought, and it makes sense. People want freedom of the mind. That is why confidence is so powerful. When we achieve this level of expression, we get closer to that freedom of the mind we yearn for. We no longer become prisoners of our minds.

When you are confident, you are also driven by a powerful human desire equal to that of transmutative energy. You gain access to those same qualities of keenness of imagination, courage, willpower, and persistence. You release inhibitions and limitations and become unstoppable through action! When you experience greater self-confidence, you experience freedom from self-doubt and negative thoughts about yourself because you live on higher vibration or state of mind. It gives you a bird's eye view of all that is possible!

When you are confident, you become a magnet attracting others towards you. They believe in you, and your connections/relationships with others become much more purposeful and meaningful. Confidence prepares you to experience life experiences at a higher level.

How you feel reflects who you are in physical form. A few months ago, I realized that I was letting myself go. It wasn't intentional; it just happened. Life got busy, and it just got easier not to worry about how I showed up. It didn't serve me because it affected me in ways I wasn't even aware of. I was depressed and felt unmotivated, which translated to a feeling of unworthiness. I was upset, frustrated, and tired all the time.

However, that is not who I was underneath it all. I love to dress up. I love how I feel when I take the time to look nice. It feels amazing. It makes me feel excited and consistently in a state of joy and empowerment, and I lose all my inhibitions. When I am in a state of mind that is so positive, I can't help but see the world through a lens of love. I am patient, loving, and understanding, and less worried about the current problems around me.

This energy not only changes how I see the world, but it also changes how the world responds to me. I harnessed this energy by bathing in the self-love of who I used to be. Now to be clear, I wasn't channeling my younger self in hopes of being like that again. I was channeling my younger self to align with that beautiful energy of confidence I had an ample supply of at that time. I was unstoppable in my early twenties. I was outgoing, full of life, and excited to be alive with my confidence. I could access my creative faculty and create the life I wanted!

I was so full of life energy that opened so many doors of opportunity for me. I was persistent in achieving whatever I goal set for myself. My courage was my superpower to being unstoppable! I wasn't afraid or intimidated to ask for the job I wanted because I was confident I would succeed at it! I was one of the youngest supervisors managing a department in a big resort at the time.

Nothing was impossible for me. I remember being so high on this energy that I would do crazy things with so much certainty and faith, such as jumping off a ledge when I bungee jumped off a 250 ft building to taking a trip to New York by myself because I wanted to see the Statue of Liberty. I wanted to experience so much, and nothing would hold me back!

The transmutative energy that aligned with my emotions reflected my confidence in my self-worth. I was on a mission to share and empower other women by feeling confident in front of the camera. Yes, I tapped into that beautiful energy, and helping others tap into this beautiful energy became my goal. The energy displayed authority, certainty, and sensuality! All the elements to represent my clients and their brand in the best way possible. This form of expression brings much success as an entrepreneur or at work. I remember being a top performer in my monthly sign-ups for the reward card at the resort I worked in. However, confidence affects relationships in all areas of our life, not just business. At the time, I didn't know it, but I was transmuting the energy into a different form of expression, and that confidence made me contagious! People felt good around me.

Reflecting on it, it wasn't the physical aspect that made me confident. Instead, it was my outlook on life.

One day I woke up and realized how uncomfortable I was in my skin; it had nothing to do with my physical aspect. It had to do with how I felt about myself. Who was I underneath all the titles and roles I currently held? I bathed myself with the memories of the young, charismatic girl I used to be many years ago. I took a negative emotion of unworthiness and turned it into a positive one of self-love. The emotion of self-love expressed in the form of confidence is powerful. In my case, it was the driving force in my desire to feel and look good, creating that confidence that influenced my world, my environment, and everyone in it.

Everyone feels it when I am vibrating at a higher level; my husband can't stop staring at me, smiling in wonder as to what is different about me. My kids take notice and feel the energy; my oldest kept telling me I looked amazing. They saw me with so much love and pride that I was their mom.

My true desire had always been to help others. At the time, helping others for me was holding space for people I with whom interacted.

Especially at work, people wanted someone to talk to and to be heard. However, I would not have fulfilled my purpose at that time if I didn't have the confidence to approach people and interact with them in a way they felt safe and comfortable. I remember people being so grateful that I would take the time to listen to their stories and make them feel like they matter; however, doing this also filled my cup. Being confident is an irresistible force that enables you to take action but also makes you a magnet for others! I have witnessed this in my life so many times.

Maintaining a higher state of vibration at all times can be difficult, but this is why we do the work. Being in a higher state of vibration allowed me to communicate with a level of confidence through the tone of my voice, being aware of the posture and carriage of my body, awareness of the vibration of thought, and taking note of my appearance, which speaks volumes and is felt so intensely by everyone who surrounds me.

When we can achieve this higher level, we fulfill the purpose of helping others along their journey. Stan Lee said it best when he coined this quote, "With great power comes great responsibility." The world is watching you. How are you showing up?

FATIMA HURD

About Fatima Hurd: Fatima is a personal brand photographer and was featured in the special edition of Beauty & Lifestyle's mommy magazine. Fatima specializes in personal branding photographs dedicated to helping influencers and entrepreneurs expand their reach online with strategic, creative, inspiring, and visual content. Owner of a digital consulting agency, Social Branding Digital Solutions, Fatima helps professionals with all their digital needs.

Fatima holds ten years of photography experience. An expert in her field, she hosts workshops to teach anyone who wants to learn how to use and improve their skills with DSLR and on manual mode. Hurd is also a mother of three, wife, certified Reiki master, and certified crystal healer. She loves being out in nature, enjoys taking road trips with her family, and loves meditation and yoga on the beach.

Author's Website: *www.FatimaHurd.com*

Book Series Website & Author's Bio: *www.The13StepsToRiches.com*

Frankie Fegurgur

MASON JARS AND TETRIS?

Before I explain why transmutation is the timeliest principle of success that you absolutely must master, I'll share how it's recently transformed my life. A week before the lockdowns started, I was driving home in the fast lane. It was dark, and traffic had slowed to a complete stop. I didn't think much of it until a few seconds later…CRUNCH! I felt my car skidding forward, with my neck whiplashed in the process. Pain shot through my entire body as I realized what had happened.

I managed to lurch into the median, thankful the other driver pulled over. They claimed to have fallen asleep at the wheel and failed to provide proof of insurance. Fortunately, they cooperated when Highway Patrol showed up. Unfortunately, in the days ahead, I was consumed with stabbing headaches, and getting around the house felt next to impossible. I sought physical therapy, only to be met with canceled appointments. The whole world was shutting down, I was in pain, and there didn't seem to be a solution. The months of inactivity started stacking up on my waistline. I'd consume sugar-filled snacks to deal with having binged on sugar-filled snacks. I packed on the pounds, fooling myself into believing each larger size of jeans was temporary. I did what I could to address the pain from the accident, but the greater problem had already burrowed its way into my mind.

For the first time in my life, I was ashamed of my weight. It affected not only my self-confidence but also my opportunities. I passed on business events, missed out on family gatherings, and continued to consume when I knew I shouldn't.

It didn't even bother me when someone I knew commented on my weight—it was nothing compared to what I would say to myself. Seeing my reflection in a store window would crush me. I began hearing thoughts like, "There's no way you can lose that many pounds," and "Maybe this is just who I am now."

Initially, I lied to myself by saying that the number on the scale didn't matter and that I was just as capable as I ever was. My faulty logic told me that if there was an emergency, I'd spring to life like the old days of being a Marine. But as the months and years went on, I couldn't fool myself anymore. I only saw my health's inevitable, cataclysmic downward spiral if I didn't act fast.

You may not relate to my specific example, but the odds are that you feel suffocated in some aspect of your life. For me, it was my weight; for you, it could be anything tied to the current state of the economy. As I'm writing this, tech companies have started mass layoffs. One social media company alone laid off 50% of its workforce in one day. Mortgage loan approvals are at their 25-year low, and 33% of small businesses are delinquent on their rent. Entire crypto exchanges are imploding in scandal. Credit card debt is nearing an all-time high, with personal savings hitting an all-time low. Inflation has potentially peaked but isn't dropping nearly fast enough for the everyday American.

No matter what year you're reading this, these types of things are always happening. Unfortunately, it's too easy to point to current events as evidence that it's not the right time to start a business, achieve financial freedom, or write your book. That's why the timelessness of this volume is so important.

You can shed the weight of emotions and beliefs that no longer serve you while redirecting that energy toward any creative expression you'd like. I'll utilize two unlikely examples of how to do this in the form of mason jars and a 1980s puzzle game. It's safe to say that most people know what Tetris is. When it hit the Nintendo GameBoy, kids and adults around the world were hypnotized. They couldn't get enough. The premise of the game is deceptively simple: Blocks fall from the top of the screen, and you rotate and slide the blocks from left to right to form a single line across the bottom. Each completed line disappears, earning you points. The simplicity of the game doesn't mean that there aren't challenges. The pieces fall faster and faster, and if you misplace them, they quickly stack all the way back to the top, ending the game. The feedback is immediate, but what is awesome is that mistakes can be resolved with the very next game piece. You can even clear multiple lines at a time, building tremendous momentum. There are parallels to the real world, but not just how you'd expect.

While you've heard of Tetris, odds are you've never heard of The Tetris Effect. People played the game for so long that it began affecting them in the real world. Players reported seeing shapes falling in front of them. Daily life became a puzzle needing to be solved. They even heard the game's soundtrack in their ears! Researchers believe this phenomenon has something to do with how our brains process thoughts and memories. This is so important because it's a perfect example of what we are wired to do. I could think of any thought, tell myself any story, and see any reality. But in the past, I chose to see all the reasons why I was overweight, so my brain went to work to find supporting evidence. Instead, I needed to redirect all those feelings that didn't serve me into flooding my brain with what my new self needed to see.

This isn't an overnight fix. It starts with becoming aware of what I want to change and then playing a different game—swap the old pieces for better pieces. If it works for countless Tetris players, it can work for anyone. Don't believe me? Have you ever been swimming, and then hours later, suddenly felt like you were still swimming? Same concept.

An even more tangible way to measure your progress is to set up two mason jars where you'll see them every day. Next to the jars, have a stack of pennies, marbles, or whatever small items you have on hand. Label the jars, one with who you were and one with who you are becoming. Stand in front of your two jars once a day or throughout the day. Pick up a penny and decide which jar to place it in. You are voting for yourself every day. You either became closer to who you were or closer to your ideal self. If you're an overachiever, use small slips of paper. Write down the action that got you closer to who you're becoming. Or, if you want to practice expressing emotion, write down the emotion you felt. Every so often, particularly when you need some motivation, read yourself those slips of paper. Acknowledge your feelings and transmute that energy into stacking more wins.

My journey is ongoing, and I started by returning to the basics. I acknowledged that I'm not 19 years old anymore, and that doesn't mean I can't still find a new level of health. A key component of this shift was accountability. I joined a group for chronic pain management and another group for better sleep. I did physical therapy through video appointments. I started volunteering in person, where I couldn't hide behind a screen. One of my favorite volunteer roles is facilitating an elementary school walking/running club. I hand out small prizes to each participant every week, hoping that one day, the kids will realize that the real prizes were the healthy behaviors and the friendships formed along the way. I also hope they learn this incredibly powerful principle of transmutation because it's not meant for one-time use or as a quick fix. It's a daily habit.

Speaking of daily habits, I also decided to stop complaining for 30 days. No judgment here, but most readers probably can't remember the last time they went a day without complaining out loud, let alone a month. At first, it took conscious effort, but after 10 days or so, I didn't even have to think about it.

The world is always changing, and we have the privilege of not only embracing but directing that change. It's time to stop hiding inside a bloated, distorted, or former shell of yourself. The world needs you. Don't allow the simplicity of my message to fall on deaf ears. Tetris is amazingly simple, and yet its effect on video gaming and culture as we know it is ever-expanding. You get to decide if you want to focus on growth or stagnation. For me, I saw and felt what the latter was like, and I have worked to shift my attitude, attention, and activities to support the upgraded me. I hope you do what's right for you.

FRANKIE FEGURGUR

About Frankie Fegurgur: Frankie's "burning desire" is helping people retire with dignity. Frankie distills the lessons he has learned over the last 15 years and empowers our youth to make better financial decisions than the generation before them. This is a deeply personal mission for him—he was born to high-school aged parents, and money was always a struggle. Frankie learned that hard work alone wasn't the key to financial freedom and sought a more fulfilling path. Now, he serves as the COO of a nonprofit financial association based in the San Francisco Bay Area, teaching money mindfulness. He, his wife, and their two children can be found exploring, volunteering, and building throughout their community.

Author's Website: *www.FrankMoneyTalk.com*

Book Series Website & Author's Bio: *www.The13StepsToRiches.com*

Fred Moskowitz

ENERGY CONVERSION THROUGH TRANSMUTATION

In looking back throughout history, we learned that the medieval science of alchemy existed with the aim of transmuting base metals into noble metals, particularly gold. But what happens when we instead consider the concept of transmuting experiences, energy, emotional responses, and feelings? Converting life's challenges, negative experiences, and troubles into something positive for us, our own unique form of beneficial 'gold'?

If you have studied the subject of Physics in high school or college, we learned early on about the concept of conservation of energy. The Law of Conservation of Energy states that energy can neither be created nor destroyed; it can only be converted from one form to another. This is what happens with transmuting thoughts and experiences: we facilitate an exchange of energy from one form into another. The skill of transmutation can be developed by working on the aspects of clarity, focus, gratitude, and emotional resilience.

Clarity

A very effective way to achieve clarity is to get out of your familiar environment and outside your comfort zone. Go somewhere new. Travel to another place alone. Have you ever done this before? I've found that is a great way to clear your mind. You have a unique opportunity to be very far away from distractions and interruptions, giving you the mental space and clarity to focus deeply, allowing thoughts and ideas to come easily and effortlessly to you.

Sometimes it is not possible to travel. Alternatively, you can stay closer to home and get out in nature for a few hours, or better yet, be outdoors for an entire day. Any amount of time is helpful, yet the more you can dedicate, the more effective it will be. This self-isolation sets the stage for some serious "thinking time."

I have had tremendous success using this tactic; whether it is getting away for a few hours or days, it works. I always come back home with a fresh perspective, having gained clarity, and coming away with new ideas that I am excited about and motivated to begin implementing.

Focus

Transmuting your emotions and feelings begins with changing your focus. When you focus on feeling good, then good things start to happen. If you find that your thoughts are not leading you down a good path, then it is critical that you immediately shift your state and your focus. An abrupt change will bring about this response. Imagine yourself plunging into a bathtub full of ice water. Will that shift your focus quickly? Absolutely it will. If you have not done it, try it and see how quickly your focus will shift.

When you constantly focus on what's going wrong or on negative things, your mind has a natural tendency to look for more of what's wrong or negative. This is part of how we are wired, as the brain always works on instinct to protect us from harm. If we do not control these thought patterns, they will continue looping with thoughts of negativity, and we will feel progressively worse. Looping thoughts circulate in a vicious cycle of self-talk that worsens as time passes; fear, anxiety, worry, despair, and helplessness can take over. The result can be a runaway freight train that is out of control.

I'd like to share with you a story. I received a telephone call one day from my friend Lenny. As we began talking, I could immediately tell from the tone of his voice that he was quite distressed and very upset. He told me about how he had gone through a recent series of unfortunate events and was starting to feel like his entire world was falling apart. Sensing his frustration and distress, I asked him if he was open to working on an analysis exercise together with me. He was open to it, and so we immediately got started. First, I had him take a blank sheet of paper and draw a line down the center of the page, from top to bottom. Then, on the left side, I instructed him to write down the bad things that had happened in his life. He listed about three or four things concerning his recent events. Then, on the right side, I instructed him to write down all the good things he had going for him. We started brainstorming.

Lenny has his health. He has all of his five senses working with full acuity. He has good technical and business skills, which are in high demand in the marketplace. He lives in a nice house in a safe neighborhood, where he lives a good life in relative peace. He has access to food, clean water, and nourishment in abundance. He has access to some of the best quality healthcare that is available. His mom is his number one cheerleader and supporter. He has family and friends that love and support him. Lenny lives in a location with nice weather for most of the year, and he loves to go outside for a walk to get outside and break up the middle of the day. He also loves stopping at his favorite cafe to pick up a hot coffee and bring it on those walks.

Within a few minutes, Lenny began to realize that he had many positive things going for him. After a couple more minutes of conversation, I could sense that he was feeling much better, and the change in the tone of his voice was dramatic.

"The most important decision we can make is whether we believe we live in a friendly or hostile universe."
~ Albert Einstein

Gratitude as a Daily Practice

Gratitude is defined as the quality of being thankful and grateful and the readiness to express appreciation for benefits and gifts received. Adopting a consistent habitual practice of gratitude is key to setting a solid foundation for the skill of transmutation. I really like the idea of being intentional with gratitude, and it is helpful to set a specific time each day to write down the top three things that you are feeling gratitude about for that day.

This is a wonderful opportunity to celebrate the wins you have achieved and write them down using pen and paper. A physiological connection is established between hand and brain when you write things down using pen and paper. When we do this, we can take a moment to savor those wins, feel gratitude, and enjoy it. The wins can be anything, small or large. Sometimes it is simply enough to write them down and silently acknowledge them that way. Other times, you might even call or text a friend to share it with them. Perhaps the celebration calls for an evening out with the family to share a nice celebratory meal. Whichever way feels right to you, be sure to celebrate your wins, and be sure to do it every day!

Gratitude helps you to focus on the good things that you have instead of focusing on what you don't have. And what we focus our attention on will expand.

Emotional Resilience

When you adopt a consistent practice of gratitude, what happens over time is that you begin to build up a high level of resilience and an ability to handle negative events, uncertainty, stressful situations, and crisis events. With this resilience, you become more adept at tackling problems and adversity and you are able to move forward effectively instead of dwelling on the fear and uncertainty that is being faced. This allows us to bounce back quickly and grow as a person.

During a negative event, we can always take a moment to acknowledge what has happened and then deliberately seek out the opportunity that is the gift for us. Then, instead of feeling that "life happened to me...," we can take the alternative position of "life happened for me...," automatically going with the presumption that there will be a benefit from what has happened—the cloud with the silver lining, as is often said.

Looking at the event or situation through a lens of curiosity, be open to asking yourself and exploring questions such as:

- What lesson is there for me to learn from this experience?

- How will I grow as a person from having successfully worked through this?

- Who are the new people that will come into my life as a result of this experience?

- Am I here to serve others or to allow someone else to serve me? Or is it both?

- What new skill or expertise am I going to get to develop here?

In summary, we can benefit tremendously from transmutation by utilizing it as a tool in any situation where we want to manage challenges, then quickly pivot or recover while experiencing growth in the process. This can be accomplished by working on the aspects of clarity, focus, gratitude, and emotional resilience.

FRED MOSKOWITZ

About Fred Moskowitz: Fred Moskowitz is a Bestselling Author, investment fund manager, and speaker who is on a personal mission to teach people about the power of investing in alternative asset classes, such as real estate and mortgage notes, showing them the way to diversify their capital into investments that are uncorrelated from Wall Street and the stock markets.

Through his body of work, he is teaching investors the strategies to build passive income and cash flow streams designed to flow into their bank accounts. He's a frequent event speaker and contributor to investment podcasts.

Fred is the author of *The Little Green Book of Note Investing: A Practical Guide for Getting Started with Investing in Mortgage Notes* and contributing author in *1Habit To Thrive in a Post-Covid World.*

Author's Website: *www.FredMoskowitz.com*

Book Series Website & Author's Bio: *www.The13StepsToRiches.com*

Gina Bacalski

THE 4 PHYSICAL STEPS TO TRANSMUTATION

Taking a break from my normal "story telling" chapter writing, I am going to instead share my very practical guide for how I physically use transmutation in my life.

Without getting too far into "woo woo" territory, a fundamental baseline of what I'm going to talk about needs to be set forth as I will be using terms in relation to what I do and how I do it. This has been around in the knowledge of man for thousands of years and it's only recently that science has started to catch up. I found a lab that can perform a scan of the human body and "prove" all of these theories, but that is neither here nor there. The point is, this stuff is real and it works if you let it.

There are seven key chakra points or energy points in our bodies. "Chakra" is Sanskrit, the official language of India, for "wheel," indicating a spinning movement.

1. Crown: The very top of the head

2. Third-Eye: Forehead between the eyes

3. Throat: The center of throat

4. Heart: Center of chest, just above the heart

5. Solar Plexus: Center abdomen, about 2 inches above the navel

6. Sacral: Lower abdomen, about 2 inches below the navel

7. Root: Base of spine, in the tailbone area

We are going to be focused on the Sacral Chakra or Energy Point and the Heart Chakra or Energy Point.

The Sacral Energy Point is where creative energy is stored and created in your body. Logically that makes sense since it is that area of the body that houses the organs that produce human life. Procreate, create.... See where I'm going with this?

The Heart is in the exact center of all the energy points in the body. This is kind of like a bridge between the three physical points (center abdomen, lower abdomen and tailbone) and the three mental/spiritual points (center of the throat, forehead between eyes, and top of head).

How I use Transmutation is broken down into four steps.

Before we start, and if you have time, do a quick Chakra Meditation so the pathways will be clear and energy will be able to flow and move freely throughout your body. A quick Google search will pull up many options but one that works for me is to sit comfortably in a quiet area. Imagine a waterfall of light pouring into the crown chakra and running down through all the energy points that I mentioned above. Focus on each area of your body for a few deep breaths and allow the light to fill the energy point and run past it to the other energy points and into the ground beneath you. I usually hold my hands over each part of my body as I allow the light-waterfall or light-fall to flow. For my tailbone energy wheel or Base Chakra, as I'm usually sitting on it, I place each hand on the tops of each thigh.

Do this mental exercise with me. It might work better if you close your eyes. I had to do so the first few times while when I was learning energy points in the body, and continue to do so from time to time as it helps me focus.

When you're ready to start, rub your hands together to wake up the chakras or energy wheels in the palms of your hands (if you're going to do a chakra meditation first, do this before you start your meditation).

1. Imagine a ball of energy gathering in your Sacral Chakra (the space below your belly button in the center of your lower abdomen). Imagine it is a ball of light, almost like a tiny sun. Place a hand over your Sacral Energy Point and imagine the ball of light or tiny sun gathering there.

2. Activate that energy and the energy wheel that houses it. Move your hand in a circular motion over the Energy Point. Tell it to activate by speaking the word "activate," either in your mind or out loud. Try to imagine or feel the warmth beneath your hands.

3. Transmutate! Now that we've gathered all that magnificent creative energy, we're gonna move it so we can more easily manipulate it and allocate it for the uses of business or art or what have you. We are going to move that ball of light up past your Solar Plexus Chakra, right above your belly button, and plunge it into the Heart Chakra, right in the center of your chest. Imagine you are pulling that beautiful tiny sun up your energy pathways to your heart. Move your hand from your lower abdomen, pulling or guiding that creative sun, up your body to the center of your chest. Do this several times. With time, if you haven't already, you'll be able to do so on one pass.

4. Be creative! Now that we have transmutated the creative energy to the Heart Chakra, you can use it! Remember how the Heart Energy Point is a bridge? Once it's there is can be used for whatever you need. What do you need creative energy for?

I usually do this exercise before I work on my novel or need to sort out a hairy business problem or before a collaborative business meeting. I've heard professional athletes do a form of this exercise before a big baseball game or a boxing match. Professional Day Traders and high-profile businessmen also do a form of this when they need to be on their A-game. More books than this one have been written about these awesome energies and abilities to use them.

Transmutation is such an interesting word, one which we don't hear too often in the present era, but one that, if we absorb the actual meaning, could have far more impact than we may currently imagine.

Here is the interesting thing, and there have been clues and hints aplenty all throughout our literature, media and cultural conversations, with one fatal flaw. What is positioned as *external* is in fact *internal*, and internal at its fundamental core: the order and operation relating to the idea and concept of genius (one who creates or discovers something that has never been before) and/or Genii (one who creates or performs something at the request of another) as it has been mythologized. Aladdin and the magic lamp, anyone?

A simple Google search into the idea of this word "Genii" will lead one to the realization of the common root with its many branches to a wide variety of creative facts. This concept is utterly fascinating when explored, but for the conclusion of this chapter, my particular focus is to connect this idea of the internal Genii or Genius that is inside everyone!

This awesome personal Genii empowers oneself to the fulfillment and the true realization to one's wishes that exacts no three-count limit. As with everything else in the chapters of this book series and the point of *Think and Grow Rich,* is to help the individual to engineer their full potential and destiny.

With mastering these steps of Energy Transmutation, I hope you will have as much success using the amazing powers of creative energy as I have over the years.

How will harnessing the awesome power of Energy Transmutation enhance your life?

GINA BACALSKI

About Gina Bacalski: Gina is a Real Estate Agent, licensed since June 2018. Her background is in Early Childhood Education where she received her Child Development Associate from the state of Utah and has an AS from BYU-Idaho. For the past 17 years, Gina thoroughly enjoyed her experience in the service industry helping families in the gifted community.

In 2019, Gina helped Jon Kovach Jr. launch Champion Circle. She brings her genuine love for people, high attention to detail, and strives to exceed client's expectations to the Real Estate industry and to Champion Circle.

Gina married the man of her dreams, Jay Bacalski, in San Diego, in 2013. The Bacalski's love entertaining friends and family, going on hikes, and attending movies and plays. When Gina isn't helping her clients navigate the real estate world, she will most often be found dancing and listening to BTS, watching KDramas and writing fantasy, sci-fi, and romance novels.

Author's Website: *www.MyChampionCircle.com/Gina-Bacalski*

Book Series Website & Author's Bio: *www.The13StepstoRiches.com*

Griselda Beck

UNLEASH YOUR CREATIVE ENERGY!

Transmutation: the transformation of energy from one form to another. Our greatest creative inspiration comes from being in a state of excitement, exhilaration, and stimulation of our senses. This elevated sensual state is how we get in touch with our "6th sense"—intuition. Creating from intuition is the most innovative tool we have and the most influential state we can embody to cause change and deep impact outside of us.

Have you ever had an extraordinary day? Perhaps from the excitement of a new love? The high of a recent achievement? The thrill of pleasure from a wild adventure like skydiving or dancing all night? Ever notice that when you're in this "great mood," not much can get you down? Traffic lights turn green, everyone seems extra nice, and you even get that free cup of coffee from the barista…just because!

It's an energy that you are emanating from this heightened feeling of bliss, and everything around you responds as if by magic. Some of your greatest ideas and "inspirations" may even come forth as thoughts or visions. Most people enjoy this "high" but don't know how, or choose not, to intentionally transform it into creating something. Many things can easily hold us back; thus, it is a practice that must be exercised and developed.

Did you know you can create this energy without needing an external stimulus to ignite it? You can also choose to be open to receiving "downloads" (aka inspiration, ideas, thoughts, visions), memorialize them, and transform those into committed action.

Harnessing transmutative energy can have incredible results:

- Companies are born this way, and innovative modalities are created

- High-ticket programs are created and filled with ease and grace

- Courageous requests are met (think salary increase, hired for a new job, asking someone for a date)

- A first date can even be a euphoric experience (immediate connection, sparks—wow!)

- Negotiations land well in your favor and preferably a win-win for all parties

- Money seems to flow out of nowhere: that unexpected check, money found, forgotten money rediscovered, bill is pardoned, etc.)

- Good Stuff! Miracles!

Typically, we count these as one-off coincidences, blessings, etc. But what if it were possible to create this whenever you wanted? What would be possible for you? What would you experience as a result?

As an intimacy coach for couples, entrepreneurs, and high-achieving women, I support women and couples to tap into this energy to create massive results in their relationships (all of them, not just romantic) and businesses. This manifestation magic became such a part of my practice as a business coach I have now chosen to focus my coaching practice in this area where results and the true desires of my clients' hearts and souls come true. This is where they connect to their purpose, their intuitive wisdom, and what I refer to as their truth.

In my event, Unleash Yourself, I had over 500 women register and experience an epic transformation. Those that joined the VIP group series created a deeper connection with themselves, enabling them to tap into their intuition, feel the power of their wisdom, create deeper trust within themselves, discover and release limiting beliefs and patterns that no longer served them, get clear on their vision and what they really want for their lives, families, relationships, and business, in a way that was so clear they could taste, touch, see, hear and smell it.

Two women created new businesses. One reinvented her business model into a profitable one and moved to a whole new state to start a life surrounded by nature, as she had been dreaming of forever. Another woman began dating, one chose to choose herself and leave her marriage, and ALL of them gave themselves permission to experiment and try new things beyond their comfort zone that LIT THEM UP! One woman was also a client with her partner. They both experienced a connection like none they had ever experienced before in their 30 years of marriage—even before having kids.

So how does one create this euphoric energy? If you're unsure what this means or if this is a new concept to you, try searching for the "emotional vibrational scale" and look at the images that come up. Here are a few tools to stimulate that creative, "high-vibe" energy:

Music is transformative: You know those songs that come on and can powerfully SHIFT your mood! You feel powerful, free, invincible, loved, vulnerable, ecstatic, euphoric, etc. So, when clients are dealing with "stuckness" or experiencing a plateau in results, I have them create their "turn on" playlist. I personally have a playlist that incites a feeling of FREEDOM without apology.

Anytime I play my own playlist, I source courage and radical authenticity! I play this before I go on stage for a keynote, facilitate a training, before a date, or during a difficult conversation, and when I'm feeling stuck energy.

My playlist contains Bon Jovi's *"It's My Life,"* Britney Spears' version of *"My Prerogative,"* EnVogue's *"Free Your Mind,"* Bette Midler's *"The Rose,"* John Legend's *"Conversations in the Dark,"* Sia's *"Unstoppable"* (my stage song) and a few Lil' Kim songs. They evoke power, freedom, authenticity, sensuality, and self-love. I play the corresponding songs depending on which feeling I get to embrace.

I absolutely love running through this exercise with my clients. The musical tastes and songs that ignite different emotions in people are as unique and vast as they are. I love watching them light up and step back into their power right before my eyes.

Meditate: Stillness and the practice of presence is a transformative tool. Admittedly, it's one of the simplest yet hardest things for me to practice. I'm up to a 20-minute meditation session now, sometimes in silence and sometimes with frequency music playing in the background. If you're new to this, start here: Begin with 3 minutes, set a timer, and work your way up to 5, 10, 20 minutes, and beyond. Journal for another 5 minutes immediately after to note any thoughts or feelings experienced and answers received.

Gratitude and Kindness: Practicing gratitude in the morning, during difficult moments, and at the end of your day support you in elevating your vibrational state. Also, practice random acts of kindness; you will see that they lift your spirits and elevate your mental state. The simplest and most profound examples are complimenting and smiling with eye contact.

"Getting into 'state,'" as coined by Tony Robbins: You can search for his 15-minute Youtube video that walks you through his process.

Physical Movement: Exercise, walking, dancing, gym, hiking…anything. It doesn't need to be long, either; just 2-5 minutes of active movement can get your blood circulating and support you in creating energy flow. The key is to get your heart pumping and be fully aware of all your senses.

The Art of Transmutation

Once you have cultivated this energy, use it! Write down ANY downloads that come to you. While in this state, write or revisit your vision, and take inventory of the things that no longer support you so you can release them and the opportunity for things that would support you. No thought or idea is too insignificant, so trust it. Even if it doesn't make complete sense in the moment, watch your inspiration make you soar!

GRISELDA BECK

About Griselda Beck: Griselda Beck, M.B.A. is a powerhouse motivational speaker and coach who combines her executive expertise with transformational leadership, mindset, life coaching, and heart-centered divine feminine energy principles. Griselda empowers women across the globe to step into their power, authenticity, hearts, and sensuality, to create incredible success in their business and freedom in their lives. She creates confident CEOs. Griselda's clients have experienced success in quitting their 9-5 jobs, tripling their rates, getting their first client, launching their first product, and growing their business in a way that allows them to live the lifestyle and freedom they want. She has been featured as a top expert on FOX, ABC, NBC, CBS, MarketWatch, Telemundo, and named on the Top 10 Business Coaches list by Disrupt Magazine.

Griselda is an executive with over 15 years of corporate experience, founder of Latina Boss Coach and Beck Consulting Group, and serves as president for the nonprofit organization MANA de North County San Diego. She also volunteers her time teaching empowerment mindset at her local homeless shelter, Operation Hope-North County.

Author's Website: *www.LatinaBossCoach.com*

Book Series Website & Author's Bio: *www.The13StepsToRiches.com*

Jason Curtis

CREATIVE IMAGINATION

"The human mind responds to stimuli, through which it may be 'keyed up' to high rates of vibration known as enthusiasm, Creative Imagination, intense desire, and so forth."
~ Napoleon Hill

JASON CURTIS

About Jason Curtis: Jason has been a serial entrepreneur for 15 years and has enjoyed serving and helping his fellow entrepreneurs build their businesses and win in this game of life—on purpose! Jason created On Purpose Coaching because he knew, through his life experiences, that he could create an impact in others. He focuses on helping his clients create better relationships with their customers. This fosters trust and rapport while generating customer loyalty.

Jason is a Navy veteran of six years. He has sailed the seas and oceans in serving his God and country. Curtis and his wife, Brianna, have been married for eight years, and they have two children.

Author's Website: *www.JasonLaneCurtis.com*

Book Series Website & Author's Bio: *www.The13StepsToRiches.com*

Jeffrey Levine

TRANSMUTING THE SMALL THINGS

I remember sitting in my office at the end of the year and thinking about what a great financial year I had had. It was the most money I had ever earned. However, I wasn't happy—in fact, I was very miserable. On my wheel of balance that I received in the mail, I wasn't doing well. I wasn't having much fun, my relationships were just okay, and my health was just okay. I also had no spiritual connection at all, and I wasn't home as much as I would've liked. I knew I needed to cut down on my seven days of working. However, I couldn't get off the proverbial cooperate treadmill.

Then, five years later, I sat in my office with heart palpitations. Because this scared me so much, I reduced my workload and started to go to the gym and work out. With my friend Neil, a bodybuilder, I started to have fun and, at the same time, get in shape. Later on, I worked out with another bodybuilder and loved every second. I loved it so much that I worked out seven days a week for many years. Because they both lifted heavy weights, I increased my strength and was in very good shape.

Because I also spent more time at home, my relationships with family improved. I felt more balanced as I started meditating and going to a spiritual center. All of a sudden, I was feeling better.

As I went on this journey, I spent more time at the gym, and it became a habit. Also, I spent more time meditating and going on many more vacations.

As one takes action instead of just thinking about it, life changes. If you find that you are stuck in certain areas of your life, just taking small steps to improve them will make a big difference.

Sometimes, the red flags take time to appear, but when they do, you will be ready to take baby steps to improve them.

Napoleon Hill's 10th step to riches is the power of transmutation. This concept is all about taking something that is negative and turning it into a positive force. It is the ability to take small steps to improve your life, even in the areas that seem insignificant. The power of transmutation is about focusing on the small things in life and using them to your advantage.

As I continued to work on my health and relationships, I started to see the power of transmutation in action. I began to realize that even the small things could make a big difference in my life. I started to focus on taking baby steps in all areas of my life, not just my health and relationships.

In my work life, I started to focus on the small things that I could do to make my job more enjoyable. Instead of just going through the motions, I started to take on new projects and challenges. I also started to look for ways to improve the processes and systems that we had in place. These small changes helped me to feel more fulfilled in my job and gave me a sense of purpose.

One of the biggest things that I learned about the power of transmutation is that it is a mindset shift. It is about focusing on the positive aspects of life and using them to your advantage. It is about taking small steps to improve your life, even if it seems like those steps are insignificant.

The power of transmutation is all about taking control of your life and making positive changes. It is about focusing on the small things that you can do to improve your life, even if those things seem insignificant. It is about taking baby steps to create a better life for yourself.

The power of transmutation is a powerful tool that can help you to create a better life for yourself. By focusing on the small things and taking baby steps, you can make positive changes in all areas of your life. It is a mindset shift that requires you to focus on the positive aspects of life and use them to your advantage. So, if you find yourself stuck in certain areas of your life, just remember that even the small things can make a big difference.

JEFFREY LEVINE

About Jeffrey Levine: Jeffrey is a highly skilled tax planner and business strategist, as well as a published author and sought-after speaker. He's been featured in national magazines, on the cover of *Influential People Magazine*, and is a frequent featured expert on radio, talk shows, and documentaries. Jeffrey attended the prestigious Albany Academy for high school and then went on to University of Hartford at Connecticut, University of Mississippi Law School, Boston University School of Law, and earned an L.L.M. in taxation. His accolades include features in *Kiplinger* and *Family Circle Magazine*, as well as a dedicated commentator for Channel 6 and 13 news shows, a contributor for the *Albany Business Review*, and an announcer for WGY Radio.

Jeffrey has accumulated more than 30 years of experience as a tax attorney and certified financial planner and has given in excess of 500 speeches nationally. Levine is the executive producer and cast member in the documentary *Beyond the Secret: The Awakening*.

Levine's most current work, *Consistent Profitable Growth Map*, is a step-by-step workbook outlining easy-to-follow steps to convert consistent revenue growth to any business platform.

Author's Website: *www.JeffreyLevine.Solutions*

Book Series Website & Author's Bio: *www.The13StepsToRiches.com*

Lacey & Adam Platt

THE ART OF TRANSMUTATION & CREATE OR DESTROY

THE ART OF TRANSMUTATION

Transmutation may sound like a big, scary word, but the concept itself is relatively simple to understand. To transmute something is really just to transfer it into something different. Think in terms of energy: If you have one unproductive type of energy, you can change it into a different type of energy. You may have heard of famous people in history who were great at this concept.

Let me explain this a little further. Have you ever gotten so mad that you just had to stand up and do something? That, very simply, is transmuting one type of energy into another. Let's take it up a step! How about when you're so angry that you have to stand up and walk around, or maybe you go wash the dishes or clean something? Are you starting to see how to change one type of energy into another?

When I started coaching years ago, I came up with a concept I call, "The Walk and Talk." Simply put, "The Walk and Talk" is something I use when people cannot figure out how to verbalize how they are feeling in a certain situation or moment.

I realized early in my personal development that I am a verbal processor —again, another fancy term for something very simple. I need to talk out my frustration, and once I do, I can create or figure out a solution to solve that problem. So, I challenged my clients to simply go on a walk and talk it out! I recommend going on a walk alone in a place where no one else is around (because you will be talking to yourself and may not want to appear crazy!). But the act of walking gets your mind and body moving; when you are in motion, you can move through the problem and find a solution.

Have you ever used the phrase "I feel stuck" or "I feel like I am hitting my head against the wall"? People say these things when they have a problem they cannot figure out a solution for. Some people find that they need to journal or write it out. This is a form of a release technique. It's also a form of transmutation! Once I have determined that my client needs to find a way to release their anger, frustration, or feeling of stuckness, I ask them some questions to figure out whether they're a verbal processor (needs to talk it out) or if they're more of a journaler (needs to write it out). Typically, most people are one or the other. However, if you find you aren't either, have fun with it and simply sing or dance!

The Art of Transmutation is the process of converting negative energy (such as anger or frustration) into a more positive and productive energy that we can use to accomplish tasks!

If you can master The Art of Transmutation, you can go from feeling stuck to being productive and calm. It really just takes choosing to convert negative energy into positive energy! So, when you find yourself stuck, ask yourself, which is the best way to work through this problem and find a solution? Do I need to talk it out? If so, go on a Walk and Talk. Do I need to invite more fun into my life? Then host a little dance party for yourself where you sing and dance around the room! Do you really need to put all of the things in your mind on paper to relieve the pressure? If you are this person, simply dump everything out of your brain onto paper. When you do this, you will find that you can prioritize or organize the things you wrote down and create a solution. Sometimes we need to be willing to write everything down to see it. Our brains like to swirl around everything that needs to get done, but we need a little organizing and prioritizing to find a solution.

It has been said that if someone can master The Art of Transmutation (typically in history), they are referred to as "genius"! They are given the title of "genius" because they are very good at converting one negative, unproductive type of energy into very productive and efficient energy. These are the type of people who get stuff done! They get stuff done in big ways!

~ Lacey Platt

YOU EITHER DESTROY OR CREATE

We all have emotions of every kind. We have emotions of happiness, sadness, anger, frustration, anxiety, stress, love, and many other emotions. When my wife and I were just getting into self-improvement, we went to a conference. At the conference, one of the presenters said, "You can take emotions and either use those emotions to destroy or create something." He went on to explain that when you get angry with your kids, you can either destroy them by tearing them down and yelling at them or go create something with that anger. Go chop some wood, build something, clean something, or work on a project. You can either get upset with your kids or do something constructive with that emotion. What the presenter said resonated with me: You can take any emotion and use that energy to destroy something or create. So, what the presenter was really talking about was the transmutation of that energy into something productive.

Think about it: You can take that anger you are feeling and either get mad at your kids or spouse, or you can go create something in the yard or build something. When you feel anxious, you can use that energy to serve others. It will take your mind off your anxiety instead of destroying yourself or your thoughts, degrading yourself to where you are crippled.

You can take the stress you feel about that paper you have to write for class and get sick about it, or you can transmute that energy and get that project done. You can take the love you feel for your family instead of thinking you will lose them or not be the person you want to be for them and transmute that energy into building a life you can enjoy with them.

The basic theme here is that you can use those emotions to destroy relationships, yourself, or something else—or you can transmute those emotions into something you will be proud of.
Stop getting lost in social media when you feel sad or stressed or have other negative emotions. Instead, create something that can help you feel accomplished and help you and those around you.

The first step to understanding this is awareness and a desire to shift from destruction to creation, just like I have many times since I learned this principle.

I'll give you an example of what I am talking about. There was a time in my life when I was super depressed and down on myself. I felt like I was not making enough money to support my family, and I felt like a failure. I was so depressed I became suicidal and felt maybe my family would be better off without me. I was in destruction mode. I got so close to taking my own life, and I knew something had to change within me. A little while after this time in my life, I learned this principle of transmuting our emotions into something positive.

This led me down a path of self-discovery and looking at how I could take those negative emotions and transmute that energy into something that would benefit myself and my family. I used that energy to return to school and get my MBA, searched for new jobs, and started making more money. Eventually, I began making more money than we ever thought possible and we recently sold our home and started traveling the country with our kids.

I had the desire to change the negative emotions I was having into something productive. As a result, we have created an amazing life for our kids where they get to see the world and learn first-hand about history and geography and hopefully experience so many amazing things in this life. This is not to say it is always easy; it can often be difficult to transmute emotions into something productive, and I'm not always perfect at it. I get mad at my kids, and I get frustrated still, but since I am aware of this ability, I can create more than destroy.

So, you have a choice to create something with your emotions. What do you want to create in your life with all the emotions you feel every day?

~ Adam Platt

LACEY & ADAM PLATT

About Lacey Platt: Lacey is an energetic, fun-loving, super mom of five! She is an Achievement Coach, Speaker and new Bestselling Author who enjoys helping everyone she can by getting to know what their needs are and then loving on them in every way that she can. Her ripple effect and impact has touched the lives of so many and continues to reach more lives every single day. Allow Lacey to help you achieve your goals with proven techniques she has created and perfected over years of coaching. Her and her husband have built an amazing coaching business called Arise to Connect serving people all around the world.

About Adam Platt: Adam is an Achievement Coach, Speaker, Trainer, Podcast Host and now a Bestselling Author. Adam loves to help people overcome the things stopping them from having the life they really want. Adam owns and operates Arise to Connect. Adam believes that connection with yourself, others, and your higher power are the keys to achievement and greater success in life. He is impacting thousands of people's lives with his message and coaching. He lives in Utah with his five daughters and dog, Max.

Author's Website: *www.AriseToConnect.com*
Book Series Website & Author's Bio: *www.The13StepsToRiches.com*

Louisa Jovanovich

PLAY FULL OUT

If you know me, you know what I believe: You can't make the wrong person right, and you can't make the right person wrong! Everyone has a role to play, and it's based on our consciousness and who we have invited to play with us.

I have come to love the space of trust and surrender.

I try to live from a place of authenticity.

At first, I didn't even know what that meant. I had to ask myself over and over again, "Is this what I really want to do? How do I really feel about this?"

Am I honoring myself right now?

I always believed that LOVE was giving more—doing more. It was not about my needs but how the other person was being cared for. Somehow that left me feeling empty, but I did not understand how. I started everything with great intentions, and then it would blow up. I did not know what it meant to give from a place that did not compromise my well-being. I felt that people would leave me if I was taking care of myself; I got comfortable with the thought of them leaving.

However, in 2022, I began to live for me. I spent 2022 LOVING ME! Giving to myself! Throughout the year, I kept asking myself these questions: "What do I want?" and "What do I need?"

I was no longer doing things from a place of anxiety or panic, but a place of calm and trust. It took a long time to feel safe.

I used to think I had to make big, confusing decisions. But all of a sudden, those got so clear, and they just sorted themselves out. All I had to do was take care of myself; it was no longer a selfish feeling but a self-love feeling.

My relationships got deeper, and how I am with everyone in my life transformed. I allow myself to love more, to give more, to be more.
I am really excited about 2023.

I have been writing my story: It's a new story. It's no longer, "What is wrong with me?" but my story gets to be, "What is right with me!?" I have discovered everything that is right with me. If we are looking for things to complain about, we will find them; if you look for things to be grateful for, you will find that.

So, this is the YEAR I'm looking for all the things I'm grateful for and all the things that are RIGHT with me.

I have been hosting a Mastermind. It has become a place for creating an extended family. A tribe where we all grow and learn from each other. It is so beautiful how much I love it. I celebrate the experience, knowing how all the beautiful soulful connections unite to create this community.

I have always felt blessed by my relationships with people. I have this ability to see the gifts and beauty in everyone. I love knowing that when we feel loved and appreciated, we light up and want to do more and be more. It seems so simple, right? It is not. I remember being a little girl and just watching people. I asked many questions because I was so curious about why people do what they do.

It is evident when someone is secure when they take action vs. when someone is insecure taking action. I wanted to know everything about how that happened. What beliefs from their childhood made them think the way they did?

I read a script describing my goals and intentions every morning. One of the things I say is that I will attract everyone I can best serve and accept them with gratitude, and we will create incredible results together. I recently added a sentence to the script that says I get to attract people who can best support me. I have to say that it has blown my mind.

Seeing how much I love being there for people brings me so much joy. This new gift of angels coming into my life and contributing to me is a new place to rejoice in. I have always felt blessed to attract people into my life and have the privilege of extraordinary experiences. To say out loud that I attract people who can best support me has been profound. As they show up, I see more clearly it is directly due to my statement. The more I am given, the more I can give. I see the value of being open and allowing such generosity.

I can't do it alone. Living in a transformed world means we all do this together. I envision happy people celebrating life, working together, and feeling so in love with each other. When we come from love, we care about how we take care of the world we live in. I honestly would not have believed this was possible before. It seemed so crazy to think people could come from love instead of fear.

I know I have made the shift, so if I could, so could everyone. I love winning; I saw how choosing courage over fear gave me the possibility. My life has transformed since.

Do you remember what you felt like growing up? I was the girl no one wanted to pick for any sport we were playing. I was afraid of the ball, and I was afraid of failing. I didn't feel confident, so I didn't play. I looked at the kids who did play, and I thought of them as leaders. I grew up still feeling just as afraid. I thought if I wanted to be successful, I would need to choose to be in relationships with the big sharks. Well, that actually scared me even more—I felt like being kind or loving would just result in my getting eaten up. Why would I want that for myself?

My daughter is in high school right now. She was just sharing with me that I tell her and her brother to be nice kids, but she said all the popular and cool kids are not the ones that are nice. It brought me back to how I felt and why I thought keeping myself small would keep me safe from the sharks.

A few years ago, I took a transformational course. I realized in that course that I was still doing the same thing—playing it safe because I was afraid of the sharks. That day, I made a conscious decision that I would never do that again. I was missing out on my life by playing it safe. I somehow decided, from that moment on, I would attract all the beautiful people in the world, play this game of trust and happiness, and share this life with them.

I have won with that decision. I am loving every moment of the very successful people in my life who are loving, kind, generous, and, most of all, are not sharks.

Living in the flow is how I would describe my life right now. I am in love with my life. The journey to the life I want is as exciting as the life I have created. I have to believe everything is exactly as it is supposed to be because it perfectly aligns with what I have always dreamed of. I celebrate the eagerness to grow, learn, love, give, and be given to.

There are true angels in this world; I feel them in action constantly. I ask a question, and the world gives me the answer. I realize my questions need to be very specific. It is how I can hear the answer when it shows up.

I am being guided. I now know and understand what it means to "play full out." I am playing to win today, in direct contrast to when I was playing not to lose before. I have to say that I am not "as" afraid—I can only say it that way for now because there are still moments I find myself afraid.

However, one big difference in my life today is that I can catch those moments and shift quickly. I feel so blessed to have this amazing opportunity to not need a rewind button, a replay button, or anything of the sort. I am so clear about who I am and how blessed I am to have lived the good and bad times. They have all shaped the person writing this chapter. I am so grateful for the opportunity to share my story. Thank you for sharing your time with me and reading it.

LOUISA JOVANOVICH

About Louisa Jovanovich: Louisa is the founder of Connect with Source. She is a mindfulness and emotional intelligence coach. She helps identify blindspots and create new beliefs which empower her clients to access a life they have never dreamed possible. She has completed 20 years of personal and transformational growth including Landmark Forum, Gratitude Training, and is a Clarity Catalyst Certified trainer. She works with entrepreneurs who seek clarity and want to up-level their lives.

Her life experiences and school of hard knocks are what make her a knowledgeable and compassionate leader and enable her to help guide others through the process of looking for answers within in order to find success and breakthrough their limiting beliefs. Her unique coaching techniques help her clients see the truth behind the stories that are keeping them stuck in the reality that they created.

Louisa is a single mother of two teenagers living in LA. Her love and compassion towards others are her superpowers, helping others reclaim their confidence, find their voice, and know their worth.

Author's Website: *ConnectWithSource.com*

Book Series Website & Author's Bio: *www.The13StepsToRiches.com*

Lynda Sunshine West

I FELT LIKE A LITTLE SCHOOLGIRL

Having run my own women's mastermind program for 6 1/2 years and teaching the *Think and Grow Rich* principles to the women in my mastermind, I still had a hard time grasping the concept of what energy transmutation is. It wasn't until I was attending the *Think and Grow Rich Tour* that I fully understood it. I heard Travon Taylor speak about energy transmutation and what it means. Travon simplified the term in such a way that I was finally able to grasp the concept. I even interviewed him on the topic.

I'm so glad I heard his speech because it enabled me to move into a different mindset. The way he broke it down helped me see that I have tremendous power within me that, when fully engaged and tapped into, can be used as one of my greatest strengths and gifts.

The way I understood energy transmutation, as Travon explained it, is that we all have this burning desire inside of us. That desire can be used for bad and for good, and the beauty of it is that we get to decide how we will use it. Then, when we know how to channel that energy from within, we can use it to get what we desire. Taking time to focus on what we desire out of life and business, and then channeling that energy into our desired results, will inevitably give us the ability to reap the rewards we want.

As I started to understand how transmutative energy can be harnessed, I started tapping into it intentionally. We can either just go through life, or we can go through life with intentionality. By knowing what we want and don't want, we can have more control over the results of our lives. Will everything turn out the way we want it to? Most likely not. But it's more likely to turn out the way we want when we know what we want and then go after it.

Having grown up in a volatile, abusive, alcoholic household, my fears were strong, and I ran away at five years old and was gone for a week (I ran to my neighbor's house, and they watched over me). When my mom found me and brought me home, I became riddled with fears and, in turn, became a people-pleaser. The people-pleaser within me didn't know how to "want" for herself. All I wanted at that time was to please everybody else so nothing bad would happen.

It was my belief that if I did or said something wrong, it would result in some sort of abuse. It's unfortunate that was my life at such a young age, but what I've learned from it has helped me to become the woman I am today. It has been through the principles of *Think and Grow Rich* that I've had a tremendous amount of growth.

I became an entrepreneur at age 51. It's one of the greatest gifts I've ever given to myself. Through entrepreneurship, I have met many incredible people who have helped me grow and learn new ways of being. Before that, I worked in the corporate environment for 36 years and had 49 jobs. As I look back on that time, it is evident to me that working for someone else was definitely not a burning desire of mine. Had it been a burning desire, I might have stayed with one job longer than 1 1/2 years. I've always had a burning desire for a better life but didn't know how I was going to have one. I kept chasing the next job and the next job and the next job, hoping that would fulfill this desire within me.

It was August 2014. I was driving to work at my 49th job, working for a judge in the Ninth Circuit Court of Appeals, when I had this epiphany: "I hate what I'm doing. I hate my life. I don't understand why I'm here.

What is my purpose? What is the purpose of this entire planet?" This is exactly what I said to myself as I pounded my hands on the steering wheel out of sheer frustration and aggravation.

When I got to work that day, I had no idea how my life would change. I was on one of those social media platforms when I saw a message from a woman who is a life coach. She said, "I'm a life coach. I took some time off, and I'm getting back into it. I'm looking for five women who want to change their lives. Is this you?" She was talking directly to me. I raised my hand and decided to work with her for five months. The transformation that came during those five months was astronomical. Working with her made me addicted to positive change, and I wanted more.

So, on January 1, 2015, I decided to embark on a journey of ridding myself of fear. Every day for 365 days, I would wake up and ask myself one simple question that would change my life: "What scares me?" I would lay in bed and wait until the first fear popped into my head. My commitment to myself was to break through that fear THAT day. You see, I realized then that fear was stopping me from living my life—and I was no longer going to let that happen.

This process of breaking through a fear every single day for a year helped me realize what I wanted out of life. It was through that process that I became motivated. Through that process, I could tap into my transmutative energy and use it to obtain the desires that were burning deep within me. I could transmute that energy to achieve a desired result. Energy transmutation is something that's deep within us. We all have it. There's no getting away from it. It's time to embrace it and discover your true desires, then go after them.

LYNDA SUNSHINE WEST

About Lynda Sunshine West: As the Founder and CEO of Action Takers Publishing, Lynda Sunshine West's mission is to empower 5 million women and men to share their stories with the world to make a greater impact on the planet. She is affectionately known as The Queen of Collaboration. Lynda Sunshine is a Book Publisher, Speaker, Multiple Times #1 International Bestselling Author, Executive Film Producer, and a Red Carpet Interviewer. At the age of 5, she ran away and was gone an entire week. She came home riddled with fears that stopped her from living and, in turn, became a people-pleaser. At age 51, she decided to face one fear every day for an entire year. In doing so, she gained an exorbitant amount of confidence and now uses what she learned to fulfill her mission. She believes in cooperation and collaboration and loves connecting with like-minded people.

Author's Website*: www.ActionTakersPublishing.com*

Book Series Website & Author's Bio: *www.The13StepstoRiches.com*

Maris Segal & Ken Ashby

THE TRIANGLE OF CHANGE

Although it may sound like it, the Triangle of Change is not a three-sided area in the ocean where ships and airplanes disappear. On the contrary, it is a place inside each of us where something new or novel appears and where three principles, working together, energy, choice, and creativity, can change or transmute any aspect of our lives into desires, goals, and manifested results. As heart-centered business consultants, coaches, speakers, and trainers, we are clearly not experts in the scientific definition of transmutation.

Science describes transmutation as what changes occur when atoms of one element are struck with particles in a linear accelerator, specifically as "fission" or "fusion." Okay, radioactive elements and linear accelerators are not concepts we work with on a daily basis. The nonscientific definition is much broader and understandable; the action of changing or a state of being changed into another form. This is where the Triangle of Change comes into play.

Change is Inevitable!

The act of changing or the state of being changed is something we all are in relationship with every day across our personal and professional lives, both on small and grand scales. Our bodies, inside and out, are in a constant state of transmutation. We are, from time to time, seized in our lives by anxiety, resentment, scarcity, and old limiting beliefs. When we wake each morning, we are not the same person we were the day before.

We are one day older; we face new challenges and have new opportunities that are unique from the previous day.

According to Scientific American, in our body, "about 330 billion cells are replaced daily, and in 80 to 100 days, 30 trillion will have replenished —the equivalent of a new you." Now that's transmutation with which we can identify. However, we don't always recognize or feel grateful for these personal transmutations.

This triangle, which is the strongest geometrical shape, connects principles over which we have complete control, our Energy, our Choices, and our Creativity! How can we change our negative energy to positive energy? How do our choices support inevitable change? How can using our innate creativity enhance our lives? This three-way relationship connects our hearts and heads, leading to personal and professional prosperity and a winning attitude of calm and compassion.

Energy Change – Energy Choice!

How we feel inside is how we show up all day. If we feel down or elated, scared or courageous, angry or peaceful, our family, friends, and colleagues can feel our energy. After 20 years of living, loving, and working together, we know first-hand that at home or at work, we can choose to shift our energy. One of the simplest ways is to look at something around which you have negative energy and convert that unpleasant feeling into something positive simply by choosing to become "curious."

Ken: Take, for example, my experience recently when Maris arranged for us to attend a culinary function. In the hours before, I found myself more interested in staying home. The book I had longed to finish and our comfortable couch were calling my name. Knowing how much this rare "date night" meant to both of us, I asked myself, "What can I look forward to at this event?" which transmuted my energy, completely shifting me from the inside! I moved from resistance to acceptance, from detached to engaged, and from indifferent to curious.

The result? We had a great evening, met amazing chefs, and tasted unique recipes created from the simplest of ingredients, ones that we use every day. Even the change in sourcing our food from farm to table is another example of transmutation.

Transmuting our energy this way aligns with a concept we teach in our coaching and training, which is "reframing." When we reframe, shifts are possible, and new possibilities emerge.

Choice Change

Maris: Another form of transmutation comes into play when we experience a very a traumatic event in our lives. For me, it was when I was living in Southern California and awakened at 4:30am by the sound of a freight train roaring through my apartment. My then-husband and I were shaken awake, as if in a shoe box, screaming in voices we did not recognize as the building tore apart, exposing the sky.

Our apartment collapsed onto the one below, leaving a pit at the end of my bed. After saving our neighbor and crawling out to safety, we stood in the street. We realized that the 6.7 magnitude earthquake had all our belongings in its darkness.

My experience in the Northridge, CA earthquake could have debilitated me for life. In the following days, as more moments of chaos and after-shocks kept us on edge, friends, and family were our strength! One of my greatest gifts was choosing victor over victim and advocating for my neighbors in the building to ensure everybody could retrieve as many of their personal items as possible from the ruins.

Being a voice of hope and empowerment transmuted this catastrophe into a new awakening and changed my life trajectory. I renewed my gratitude for living and my commitment to creating connections, experiences, and impact versus collecting stuff. For you, maybe it's a car accident, a hurricane, job loss, or the untimely passing of a loved one. Using the experience constructively and not getting stuck in victimization is the power of choice transmutation.

We are all making choice transmutations moment by moment. We are not talking about decisions; we are talking about what precedes decisions. So, what comes before a decision is choosing what you want. If we are clear on what we "want," then there may be a number of paths to take that will manifest that "desire." We make choices not just based on the "pros" and "cons." We also follow an instinctual calling, an alluring voice leading us toward our desires. Choices don't always have a happy ending.

However, when we choose our direction, we can't blame not having all the factors for a decision. When we spend all our time in our heads and fail to listen and trust our hearts, that voice inside, and our deepest vibrations, we can just spin the wheels of analyzation and never move beyond the starting line. When we choose to stand up and step forward to engage, choose to be all-in, and choose to be curious, then possibilities become available from the transmutation of choice!

Creative Change

We've saved the most fun for last, and that's the power that lives in "creative" transmutation! Nothing man-made exists that wasn't born from someone's creativity and imagination. Creativity is the playground of the mind!

Over our many years as executive event producers and relationship-centered business consultants, working with heads of households to Heads of State, we have been honored to help lead a number of iconic historical and cultural commemorations. At the core of each was a collective commitment to be inclusive and true to the often-ugly history and a willingness to use creative approaches to engage people of all ages in understanding America's milestones.

How did we do this? Working with historians, leaders, and experts, we explored the early beginnings of America and the stories of influence and injustice of the Native Americans and the African Americans and transmuted their often-painful stories and raw facts into a series of contemporary, historically accurate experiences. We created exhibitions and narrative productions, musical and live stage performances, classroom programs, and a television special that engaged millions while honoring the impact of their contributions to the building of America.

Ken: As a singer/songwriter since my teens, I understand the power of creative transmutation. From the moment an idea for a song shows up, the idea of creative change is undeniable. A line or phrase, read in a newspaper or magazine, or an emotion or thought that just comes through me triggered from a past drama, can launch my creative juices and propel me through iterations of the lyrics.

Then, developing the melody that feels connected to the lyric is an energetic change personified. I keep open to change by playing with this note or another until the harmony of the lyric and melody resonates.

We can create the indispensable synergy which can open doors and unlock potential in every aspect of our lives. Applying the concept of transmutation using The Triangle of Change, our energy, choices, and innate creativity are all tools to keep our hearts and head working together to deliver on our desires.

Deepak Chopra said this: "By making conscious choices in our behavior and where we focus our attention (energy), we can transform our experience of our body, decrease our biological age, and tap into our inner reservoirs of unbounded energy, creativity, and love." Our inherent abilities, and higher mental vibrations, is a superpower that is constantly available to each of us.

MARIS SEGAL & KEN ASHBY

About Ken Ashby & Maris Segal: From Mindset to Marketing, Ken Ashby & Maris Segal, a husband and wife dynamic duo, have spent the last thirty-plus years bringing an innovative, collaborative voice to issues, causes, and brands. As entrepreneurs, activists, business strategists, executive producers, coaches, authors, speakers, and trainers, Ken & Maris work with the public and private sectors from boardrooms and classrooms to the world stage. They are known for creating high-touch experiences that unite diverse populations across a broad spectrum of business, policy, and social issues. Their leadership expertise in Business Relationship Marketing, Organizational Change & Cultural Inclusion, Personal Growth, Project Management, Public Affairs, and Philanthropy Strategies has been called upon by companies and their agencies. Their experience includes: consumer and financial brands, Olympic organizers, Super Bowls, America's 400th Anniversary, Harvard Kennedy School, Archdiocese of LA and NY Papal visit planners, the White House and celebrities across the arts, entertainment, sports, and culinary genres.

With Ken's expertise as an award-winning singer-songwriter, they launched ONE SONG, a songwriting workshop series designed to unleash creativity in individuals and teams. Their **DRIVE** method: **D**esire, **R**elationships, **I**ntention, **V**ision and **E**mpowerment sits at the core of their companies Prosody Creative Services, ONE SONG, and Segal Leadership Global to set a path for every client to Build High Performing Businesses & Elevate Personal & Professional Leadership for Maximum Impact & a 360-degree Thriving Life!

Author's website: www.SegalLeadershipGlobal.com

Book Series Website & Author's Bio: *www.The13StepsToRiches.com*

Mel Mason

GOOD VIBRATIONS AND TRANSMUTATIONS

"A willingness to examine ourselves is the first step toward increasing our vibration frequency."

In October 2021, I nearly died in a car accident that was my fault. I was driving down a mountain road, testing out my new tires, going faster than I should when I veered just a little too far to the right. The slight deviation onto loose gravel sent the truck airborne. Turns out new tires don't do much for you unless they're touching the ground.

In a flash, the truck flipped over—once, twice, maybe a third time. In the chaos, I couldn't be sure. I braced my hands against the roof of the car, thinking I'd be able to prevent my head from slamming against the top of the car as it was airborne. The realization hit that I was probably about to die, and rather than a rush of adrenaline, a wave of deep calm settled over me.

Then the world stopped spinning. The air was quiet as if the wildlife alongside the road had witnessed the accident and were stunned into silence. I blinked a few times, unsure. The truck was right side up. On the side of the road. Not, as I had expected, upside down and in flames. No, I was in my truck, the right way up, now facing the road I had just driven down.

Aware of the dangers of staying in a recently crashed car, I scrambled to get out of the truck, kicking the driver's side door open. All the windows had shattered, but I didn't have a scratch on me. Stepping out of the truck, I could see it was totaled. My legs suddenly felt like they were made of Jell-O.

My belongings and broken glass littered the roadside: my travel mug, a mini first aid kit, a sweatshirt, the truck's manual, and an unopened plastic water bottle. I plucked up the first aid kit and the travel mug, hands shaking. I tucked the objects under my arm. Picking up the sweatshirt, a shard of glass fell from the folds and nicked the ring finger on my left hand. Red-rose blood formed at the site of the cut. Then, it hit me: Miraculously, I was alive.

2021 was a year of self-sabotage for me. In a post-divorce haze, I started drinking excessively, picked up a smoking habit, and self-isolated, which only worsened my loneliness and self-pity. All year I had struggled with the belief I didn't deserve to live. The crash wasn't intentional, but I knew I sourced the experience as the beginning of my process of transmutation.

Transmutation is the changing or transforming of one form of energy into another. Transmutation allows us to move from a low-energy state to a higher state. For me, transmutation began when I remembered that circumstances in life are a direct reflection of the energy a person emits. After the crash, I saw through the pain and limiting beliefs I was clinging to for most of the year. I did, in fact, want to live—I deserved to live.

Most crashes on that mountain road end with a car in a ball of flames, yet, I had walked away with a single scratch. I finally looked at my behavior, examined it, and began transmutation from the low-frequency life I was leading to the high-frequency life I lead today.

I speak with clients about the three vibration frequencies: low, middle, and high. They each correspond to a certain perspective on life. People who emit low-frequency vibrations usually view life as something that happens to them. Often, they are stuck in a victim mindset. They believe their situations are never their fault, even if originating from their choices.

Low-frequency vibrations mean a person sees life in binaries. It is rigid, with hard-set rules and defined winners and losers. There is no such thing as a win-win world for someone who is vibrating at a low frequency.

Additionally, people leading low-frequency lives tend to attract other low-frequency people and events into their lives. They do this to confirm their victimhood and hide from their pain. They are unwilling to look at their own lives and instead distract themselves by seeking out the next outside threat.

The middle range frequency has a worldview that says life happens for me. While it is a more positive outlook, it is a belief that still denies a person has any responsibility for their life. If life happens for you, there is not much you can do to change what comes your way. People in a middle range frequency may become frustrated when facing challenges because they still blame the world for what they are given, both the positives and the negatives.

At a high frequency of vibration, a person knows that their life is created vibrationally. When an individual emits a high-frequency vibration, life is easier because they take responsibility for their actions and reactions. They understand any problems are signs pointing them to look more closely at their lives, and that pain and challenges are opportunities to discover nuanced answers rather than black-and-white ones.

At higher frequencies, living is easier and requires less effort. Anxiety falls away. Emitting a high-frequency vibration means temptations are easy to resist. It becomes second nature to say 'no' to a sweet treat, a toxic love affair, or the urge to send a vindictive email reply. Existing at a high frequency, individuals' reactions to outward stimuli change because they welcome and take responsibility for whatever enters their lives. The pastry shop is forgotten altogether. The lovers fade out of each other's lives to focus on themselves. The initial email doesn't appear offensive.

These three types are a spectrum rather than three set levels. Through transmutation, we can shift from low to medium to high vibration frequencies. In working with clients, I've discovered a willingness to look at oneself is key to transmuting from one frequency to another.

By the same token, avoiding honesty and introspection transmutes a higher frequency to a lower one. We can change a low-frequency victim mindset to a wise, high-frequency understanding through deep self-compassion and honesty. As I tell my clients, we are the sole, uncontested authors of our lives.

However, some people can be successful while operating at a low frequency. People have mounted careers on a low-frequency vibration. The problem is that low-frequency states are taxing, stressful, and inherently self-defeating. When individuals refuse to look inward and reject responsibility, they give away their power to lead a better life.

Moreover, low-frequency vibrations attract increasingly more victim-affirming situations until the individual has no choice but to confront what they have tried to avoid. After my accident, I could have continued to blame, rant, and self-destruct until an even worse accident occurred. But instead, I willingly looked at my self-destructive behavior, limiting beliefs about my worth and victimhood, and opted to take responsibility for my behavior for the previous nine months. I came to understand it was time to let go of the hurt and pain I associated with my ex-spouse—it wasn't serving me.

Instead, it blocked me from experiencing new love and joy. The truck, which we bought while we were together, was the last possession I had from the marriage. It was time to let it go—the truck, the pain, the self-sabotage. I could have let it destroy me, but instead, I allowed it to save me. After the accident, I stopped smoking and drinking. A month later, I joined a walking group, which in a few months transmuted into training for a marathon.

The power of transmutation, when shifting from low to high frequencies, is an experience with less strife, anxiety, and frustration. It's not that someone operating at a high-frequency vibration will never encounter pain or hardship. Rather, the pain and hardship are less daunting, less sharp, and less stressful.

For example, this past year, I enjoyed a vibrant new friendship. We went from being mere acquaintances to speaking or messaging almost every day. Six months later, I noticed she and I hardly messaged at all. Neither of us had ghosted the other. We never officially ended the friendship. We flowed into one another's lives, enriched our experience, offered support, and, reaching a fork in the river, flowed into separate channels. There was no animosity, just a mutual understanding that life takes us in different directions.

I could have taken our drifting apart as a personal affront, chased the relationship, or exerted more effort to maintain it. Instead, at a high-frequency register, I was grateful for her to be in my life in the first place and have let go of what is no longer needed. Sometimes, at low frequencies, a person can spend so much time clinging to pain or blame they forget what it's like to live without it.

If stuck at a low frequency, we can begin transmutation with a single instance of sincere self-examination, even if it feels like a small or trivial incidence. These tiny moments of transmutation are practice for the times when self-reflection or letting go will be more difficult. If we can cultivate the willingness to look and look again, a life full of good vibrations is within reach.

MEL MASON

About Mel Mason: International Bestselling Author Mel Mason is The Clutter Expert, and as a sexual abuse survivor, she grew up depressed, suicidal, and surrounded by clutter. What she realized after coming back from the brink of despair and getting through her own chaos was that the outside is just a mirror of the inside, and if you only address the outside without changing the inside, the clutter keeps coming back. That set her on a mission to empower people around the world to get free from clutter inside and out, so they can experience happiness and abundance in every area of their lives.

She is the author of *Freedom from Clutter: The Guaranteed, Foolproof, Step-by-Step Process to Remove the Stuff That's Weighing You Down.*

Author's Website: *www.FreeGiftFromMel.com*

Book Series Website & Author's Bio: *www.The13StepsToRiches.com*

Miatta Hampton

PURE GENIUS

"A better definition of a genius is 'an individual who has discovered how to increase mental intensity and concentration to the point where he or she can freely communicate with sources of knowledge not available through ordinary levels of thought.'"
~ Napoleon Hill

MIATTA HAMPTON

About Dr. Miatta Hampton: Dr. Miatta Hampton is a nurse leader, #1 Bestselling Author, speaker, coach, and minister. Miatta impacts others with her powerful, relatable messages of pursing purpose, and she empowers her audiences to live life on purpose and according to their dreams. She coaches and inspires women to turn chaos into cozy, pivot to prosperity, and how to profit in adversity. Miatta provides tools and resources for personal, professional, and financial growth.

Author's Website: *www.DrMiattaSpeaks.com*

Book Series Website & Author's Bio: *www.The13StepsToRiches.com*

Michael D. Butler

TRANSMUTATION AKA TRANSFORMATION

Growing up on the farm in Oklahoma was a boring life for some kids, but for me it opened up a whole new world of wonder and amazement. Everything was new, different, and waiting to be explored by me and my brother. We were the Tom Sawyer and Huck Finn of our county and we came home nightly with tales of adventure equal to the folklore we read in the classics—at least in our own minds.

My sense of optimism came from my parents and my uncle: My parents for their hard work, moral values and strict discipline and from my uncle because of the books he bought for us.

My uncle had just graduated from Dale Carnegie's Speaker Training, and this—coupled with his addiction to Earl Nightingale's audio cassettes from such authors as Denis Waitley, Jim Cathcart and W. Clement Stone —not only put my uncle on a life-long quest of being a book lover but being a student of personal development. He was ready to take on the world! He just turned 90 and he still reads 3 books a week and does 100 push-ups and 50 sit ups per day.

Every birthday and Christmas, he'd load me and my brother up with interesting books about all topics, from sports to hunting, to politics, to history and biographies—he brought us everything! And this is where I first heard the term transmutation.

Transmutation, as described by Napoleon Hill, is the process of converting negative energy into positive energy. It involves taking negative emotions, such as fear or anger, and transforming them into positive ones, such as courage or determination.

But the way I remembered the word as a 12-year-old boy was to tie it to the word "TRANSFORMATION" and I found the scripture in Romans 12: 2: "And do not be conformed to this world, but be transformed by the renewing of your mind...."

According to Hill, transmutation is a key factor in achieving success in any area of life. By learning to control our thoughts and emotions, we can channel them towards productive ends and use them to fuel our ambitions.

For example, if we experience fear or doubt about a particular goal or task, we can transmute that negative energy into determination and perseverance. We can use the energy that was once holding us back to push ourselves forward and achieve our desired outcome.

Ultimately, transmutation is about taking control of our own minds and emotions and using them to our advantage. It requires practice and discipline, but the rewards can be significant, leading to greater success, happiness, and fulfillment in life.

Using Transmutation in My Own Life to Overcome 3 Very Real Fears

Public Speaking: Many people experience fear or anxiety when speaking in public. Instead of letting this fear hold them back, they can use transmutation to channel that nervous energy into a more positive emotion, such as excitement or enthusiasm. By focusing on the positive aspects of the speech, such as the opportunity to share valuable information or connect with the audience, individuals can overcome their fear and deliver a successful presentation.

Entrepreneurship: Starting a business can be daunting and overwhelming, leading to fear and self-doubt. However, by transmuting these negative emotions into determination and confidence, entrepreneurs can push through their fear and take the necessary risks to succeed. By focusing on the potential rewards and the opportunity to make a positive impact on the world, entrepreneurs can use their fear as a motivator and achieve their goals.

Fitness: Many people feel intimidated or fearful when starting a new fitness routine or workout program. However, by transmuting that fear into excitement and determination, individuals can push through their initial discomfort and achieve their fitness goals. By focusing on the positive benefits of exercise, such as improved health and energy, individuals can use their fear as a catalyst for positive change and achieve lasting results.

Graduating and Growing to New Stages

Life is about growth and development. Challenges help us grow. Every new stage requires things from us that we did not have in the previous phase. Pain brings change. We can choose to evolve in our pain and change our thinking and our course of action, or we can curse our circumstances and hope for better days.

The patient and persistent farmer who plants seeds, knowing his family and friends will be sitting around his table during harvest, also knows that those who were too lazy or cynical to plant will beg for food and have none.

Decide to transform individually on the inside today and watch what happens around you, for you and for others!

MICHAEL D. BUTLER

About Michael D. Butler: Called the Simon Cowell of Book Publishing, celebrity kingmaker Michael Butler is most proud of his 4 sons and 2 grandsons. As a global book publisher with 749 titles by authors in 49 countries, Butler is a recognized authority in the book publishing space. He helps authors and speakers evolve and create platforms of influence in an ever-changing marketplace.

Author's Website: *www.MichaelDButler.com*

Book Series Website & Author's Bio: *www.The13StepsToRiches.com*

Michelle Cameron Coulter & Al Coulter

FROM ATHLETES TO ENTREPRENEURS: TRANSMUTATION OF LESSONS LEARNED

Hey there! Today we want to talk to you about something called "transmutation." It's a fancy word, but it just means turning a bad thing into a good thing. In sports, we've learned a lot about teamwork, discipline, focus, resilience, finding a way, always growing, constantly improving, and overcoming challenges. And guess what? These lessons can be applied to other areas of our lives too, such as relationships, careers, and personal growth.

In this chapter, we're going to show you how the lessons we've learned in sports can help you succeed in entrepreneurship. We believe that perseverance, teamwork, discipline, focus, and resilience are key skills that can be applied in any area of life. We'll share our personal stories to show you how these lessons can be transmuted and applied in different ways to achieve success in both sports and business.

As Olympic athletes, we've experienced both the highs and lows of sports. We've won and we've lost. One thing we know for sure is that the lessons we've learned in sports have helped us in our careers as entrepreneurs.

For me, Michelle, becoming a World Champion and Olympic gold medalist in synchronized swimming was a long and tough journey. I failed my first level of swimming lessons four times before finally achieving success. These experiences taught me an important lesson about perseverance and resilience. In sports and in business, you might face setbacks or failures, but it's important to keep trying and never give up on your dreams.

I used this lesson in my career as an entrepreneur, where I started a successful speaking and retreat business called Gold Medal Inspirations. I knew that success would not come overnight, but with hard work, determination, and a willingness to learn from my mistakes, I could achieve my goals.

As for me, Al, I learned a lot about teamwork and discipline during my career as an Olympic volleyball player. In volleyball, you must work together with your teammates to score points and win games. This same teamwork is essential in business, where you might have to work with a team of employees or collaborate with other businesses to reach your goals.

I also learned about focus and resilience during my career in sports. In order to succeed in volleyball, as well as take on the leadership role of the captain for Team Canada, I had to stay focused on my goals and keep practicing even when things didn't go as planned. I used this same focus and resilience in my career as an entrepreneur, where I started a successful construction and renovation company.

"Resilience" means not giving up, even when things are hard. Both Michelle and I had several attempts to make our teams on every level leading up to our National teams and then eventually on to the Olympics. One of Michelle's favorite quotes that always kept her going is, "Good Timber does not grow with ease; the stronger the wind the stronger the trees." This quote reminds us to just keep trying, learning, and growing, even if you miss a few times. That can help you in life too when things don't go as planned.

We both believe that the skills we learned in sports have helped us become successful entrepreneurs. Here are some of the lessons we learned that can be applied to any area of life:

Perseverance and resilience: Whether you're playing sports or starting a business, there will be setbacks and failures. But it's important to keep trying and never give up on your dreams. Use your failures as opportunities to learn and grow.

Teamwork: Success is rarely achieved alone. Surround yourself with a team of people who share your vision and work together to achieve your goals.

Discipline: In order to succeed, you must be disciplined and focused on your goals. This means setting priorities, managing your time effectively, and staying motivated even when things get tough.

Focus: In sports and in business, it's easy to get distracted by the noise and lose sight of your goals. Stay focused on what's important and don't let distractions get in the way.

Resilience: Life is full of challenges and obstacles. But by staying resilient and persevering through difficult times, you can overcome any obstacle and achieve your goals.

We have used these lessons in our own lives to achieve success in both sports and business. For example, Michelle used the tools she learned from overcoming her fear of water and failing her swimming lessons four times in every area of her life, from raising a family and navigating a 30-year marriage together, to being an entrepreneur.

Allan, as well, used the teamwork and discipline he learned in volleyball to build a successful construction company that has been in business for over 30 years.

Transmutation is a powerful tool that can be used to turn a negative experience into a positive one. As athletes, we've learned to apply this tool in our lives both on and off the courts and pools. We've learned that setbacks and failures are opportunities for growth and that by staying focused on our goals, we can achieve success in any area of our lives.

So, whether you're an athlete, an entrepreneur, or just someone looking to improve your life, remember that the lessons of transmutation can help you reach your full potential. By turning negative experiences into positive ones and by staying focused on your goals, you can achieve success in whatever you choose to do.

MICHELLE CAMERON COULTER & AL COULTER

About Michelle Cameron Coulter: Michelle is an Olympic gold medalist, entrepreneur, mother of four, community leader raising millions of dollars for charities, global inspirational leader, and founder and CEO of Inspiring Possibilities.

About Al Coulter: Al is a two-time Olympian in volleyball, captain of Team Canada, world record holder in matches representing one's country in any sport, with over 735 matches, entrepreneur, father of four, and personal best coach, specializing in relationships, team, and resilience.

Michelle and Al are the embodiment of today's leaders. Strong and empowering, they embraced life's challenges with strength and courage. They bring insight, compassion, depth, and inspiration to the table with multiple world championships, three Olympics, an Olympic gold medal, marriage, and four children.

They are sought-after inspirational leaders. Through their speaking, workshops, and retreats, their gift and passion is to "inspire possibilities" and encourage people to embrace their greatness in a real, authentic, healthy, and vibrant way—creating thriving community, connection, and one's own gold medal results.

Author's Website: *www.MichelleCameronCoulter.com*

Book Series Website & Author's Bio: *www.The13StepsToRiches.com*

Michelle Mras

I AM WOMAN

When I was a little girl in the Philippines, my grandfather sat me on the ground and explained to me that we are all energy. He guided me to pray to connect with spirit and God. He had me focus on the warmth from the ground and feel it travel through my body into my heart. That was when I was to pray and connect directly to the source. This exercise in energy and spiritualism was my introduction to transmutation.

Later, as a teenager, I read, *Think and Grow Rich.* When I reached the chapter regarding Transmutation, the song, *I Am Woman,* by Helen Reddy was popular. The correlation didn't dawn on me then, but as I prepared to write my perspective of this chapter, the Helen Reddy song continually popped into my thoughts:

> *"I am woman; hear me roar in numbers too big to ignore*
> *and I know too much to go back and pretend.*
> *Cause I've heard it all before, and I've been down there on the floor.*
> *No one's ever gonna keep me down again.*
> *Oh yes, I am wise. But it's wisdom born of pain.*
> *Yes, I've paid the price. But look how much I gained.*
> *If I have to, I can do anything...*
> *I am strong (strong)*
> *I am invincible (invincible)*
> *I am woman."*

The embodiment of owning my presence, in conjunction with what my grandfather taught me, helped me realize that all energy can be shifted. From these two lessons, I created and led training regarding this shifting of energy to create a self-serving superpower.

Have you ever been in a room and felt someone walk in? They don't need to make a sound; their very presence changes the energy in the room. Many call it charisma; I call it the perfect example of the essence of energy transmutation. Those with this quality have learned to own their space. They have created an art of transmuting their energy to draw to them anyone in their path.

Women who are phenomenal examples of this attitude are Sophia Loren, Dion Warwick, Hedy Lamarr, Eartha Kitt, Julie Andrews, Nichelle Nichols, Lucille Ball, Princess Diana, and Barbara Bush, to name a few. Each of these women created success by utilizing their magnetic energy, their comfort of being a woman, and knowing that attraction comes not from an outward physical appearance. The appeal of these women radiated from their essence of not apologizing for their sex, color, stature, social background, spouses' position, or public opinion. In my humble opinion, that is a superpower!

Another example of the transmutation of energy is personal magnetism. I speak about the power of personal magnetism in my training, *Amplify Your Magnetism*. Essentially, how to turn on and increase your personal charisma to attract what you want.

Transmutation is beyond the physical aspect of attraction. It is a shift of the physical to the mental capacity to attract what you desire in life. Through developing your magnetism and charisma, you purposefully activate your transmutation energy of attraction on a base level of awareness of self, ownership of who you are as an individual, and the energy you emit as a being of love, light, and goodness.

What does this involve? How can you, as a reader, activate this basic step of energy transmutation? The following are basic tools to amplify your magnetism which, in turn, switches your energy transmutation on. A song helps shift your mindset into a positively charged "can do" attractor.

Have you ever been in a bad mood, then got into your car and heard your favorite upbeat song? Remember that moment. Were you able to stay in your bad mood? More than likely not. You begin to sing along, tap your feet, and forget your negative mindset.

Music is a powerful tool. Why is that? We are programmed from before birth to respond to a beat—our mother's heartbeat, the movement of her blood through her veins, and the muffled sounds from outside the serenity of her womb.

So, when we are now outside the protection of our mother's body, our minds seek solid, familiar… music. The next is to do what the women I listed above managed to do: They owned their space and never apologized for being who they were.

Energy transmutation is not a physical shift. Transmutation is defined as "the action of changing or the state of being changed into another form." In this case, we are talking about the mental shift that occurs when a person no longer succumbs to the physical aspect of this human experience.

Energy, by definition, cannot be destroyed; it can only be converted. The energy transmutation we speak of is a conversion of physical energy to be applied to fuel one's thoughts, creativity, and pursuits for success.

Let's look at the development of a relationship. New relationships are a perfect analogy for what occurs with energy transmutation. You meet someone, and there is an instant feeling of wanting. As you learn more about that person, you become obsessed; you get home and can't stop thinking of them, the sound of their voice, their smell, how they walk, their laugh, the way their hair falls across their face when they laugh— you know the pattern.

You can see, smell, taste, and experience everything about them within your mind. You pursue them by being the best version of yourself. You pay attention to their every need. You court them by giving attention, spending quality time, and providing undivided attention. Together you dream of the life you will build together. If these dreams align, you create a life together.

This is energy transmutation: You focused all your energy on obtaining the relationship, courted another into the same end game, and it became a reality. The same conversion can happen with any object, goal, or achievement you truly desire. Focus on it. Dream of it. See, taste, smell, and live as you already know your end game. That focused excitement is the transfer of energy into reality.

The transformation of energy is most often used unintentionally. As we have discussed throughout this series of *The 13 Steps to Riches*, this energy must be focused on with intentionality. What do you want? Focus on it as if it were a relationship you long for and if you can channel that excitement of your desire into an insatiable determination…you will have achieved energy transmutation.

MICHELLE MRAS

About Michelle Mras: Michelle is a Global Award-Winning Keynote & TEDx Speaker, Presentation Coach, Co-Host of two podcasts: Denim & Pearls and Amplifluence. Michelle is the Host of MentalShift on The New Channel (TNC), Philippines. She's a multiple Bestselling Author and Co-Founder of Amplifuence - Amplifying the influence of Coaches, Authors and Speakers.

Michelle is a survivor of multiple life challenges to include a Traumatic Brain Injury and Breast Cancer. She guides others to recognize the innate gifts within them, stop apologizing for what they are not and step into who they truly are… Unapologetically.

Author's Website: *www.MichelleMras.com*

Book Series Website & Author's Bio: *www.The13StepsToRiches.com*

Mickey Stewart

BACKSTAGE PASS TO COMING ATTRACTIONS

While I type these words, I'm looking at the cover of one of my notebooks that contains the well-known quote, "Energy flows where attention goes." In my opinion, this quote is the shortest, quickest, and easiest way to summarize the process of transmutation. If I could add one adjustment, it would be, "Energy flows where attention goes—when supercharged by desire."

In this discussion on transmutation, "the changing or transferring of one element, or form of energy, into another," as Napoleon Hill defined it, I'm going to laser in on my favorite form of transmutation, the one by which I live my life and of which I have decades of proof: The transmutation of thoughts into physical reality.

When I was eight years old, I watched a sitcom called *The Facts of Life*. It was about girls living at a boarding school, and oh, how I thought that would be fun and exciting. Decades later, I would get to experience my own boarding school scenario, but this time as a teacher rather than a student.

The icing on the cake was that, instead of taking place in New York State, my real-life sitcom was set in the Scottish Highlands, at my very own version of Hogwarts. Instead of the house names like Gryffindor,

Hufflepuff, Ravenclaw, and Slytherin, they are Barrie, Burns, Buchan, and Scott. And I teach drumming rather than magic.

As I wheeled my music bag to the car after a full day of drum lessons, one of my young students shouted from an upstairs window, in a posh Scottish accent, "Hello, Mrs. Stewart!" I replied, "Hi, Charlie!" Then I heard him say to his friends, "That's Mrs. Stewart. She's so cool." I smiled and laughed to myself as I turned away because I've always felt like Jack Black's character from *The School of Rock* and hoped I inspired my students with the same contagious enthusiasm as Mr. Finn. So, when I heard Charlie's comment to his classmates, I knew I was hitting the mark.

So, how do our thoughts transmute into things or reality? All thoughts and emotions carry their own vibrational or wave frequency, with the length and height of each frequency correlating to the degree of energy they possess. Science backs this up, and although I enjoy "geeking out" over the scientific facts, I find real-life, relatable human experiences to be my preferred form of evidence and more inspiring to read about.

Transmutation is happening all around us, constantly, throughout the day. For example, we have a portable gas fire in our third-floor creative space, where we play and compose music, write books, hold online meetings, record audio and videos, practice yoga, etc. This portable gas fire transmutes gas into heat so that we don't have to turn the main boiler on, which would heat all three levels of the house when we only need warmth in one room.

I can jump in the car to run to the shops and Ta-Da! With the turn of a key, the petrol in the tank is converted from chemical energy to heat energy to mechanical energy. I don't have to be an electrician or mechanic to take advantage of these everyday transmutations.

Just like you, I covered the basics of this in school, but even if I was brought up by a pack of wolves in the woods, if I found a cabin in those woods and turned the light switch on, the lights would still come on without any understanding of how it worked.

You wouldn't refuse to use every appliance you could access just because you didn't understand how it worked. If you went to someone's house and they said, "This Vitamix can take big chunks of carrots and blend them into hot soup," you wouldn't say, "I don't understand how that works, so I don't believe in it."

But what if your friend explained the machine uses friction energy to heat the soup, just like how you heat your cold hands by rubbing them together? Does it work any differently? No!

You don't have to understand how the world of quantum mechanics and metaphysics works to enjoy their benefits. Just as a liquid can transmute to ice or steam, the fact that you can't see moisture in the air doesn't mean it doesn't exist.

Think of your imagination as a Human Thought Dehumidifier, except instead of converting humidity from the atmosphere into liquid $H2O$, it takes your thoughts (formless) and transmutes them into reality (form).

Thinking thoughts without a strong desire and expecting them to become a reality is like expecting an unplugged dehumidifier to work. Once you add this secret ingredient, the conversion can then begin. Add a few extra scoops of belief in there, and you're on your way.

In the Spring of 1989, I found myself in a puddle of tears, crying my eyes out in the bathroom stalls of the Rebecca Cohn Auditorium in Halifax, Canada. I wanted to study music, but after my auditions and theory tests, I realized this was not the music I yearned to study. I thought I had my life planned out, at least for the next few years. But my dreams came crashing down all around me.

With every fiber of my being, I wished there was a place that specialized in Traditional Scottish Music. If I knew the Royal Scottish Academy of

Music and Drama existed, I would have done anything to go there as a student.

Years later, that powerful wish, felt with one of the most intense emotions I ever experienced, manifested itself into a teaching position through Glasgow's Royal Scottish Academy of Music and Drama's Youthworks program. I wanted to study there but ended up teaching there!

Earlier, at age sixteen, I dreamed I would marry American singer-songwriter Randy Travis and become his drummer. A year or two later, I found myself wandering around backstage (somehow with a crew all-access backstage pass) at one of his concerts, where I met and had my photo taken with the country legend himself. A good bagpiping (and composer) friend was so surprised to discover this self-proclaimed Trad music snob was also a country girl at heart that she wrote a tune for us called *Mickey and Randy*.

Years later, in 1997, on a snowy Robbie Burns Night, just after serving the haggis, another good friend (who also published this tune in one of his piping books) read a congratulatory telegram from Mr. Travis himself at my wedding reception. I don't have confirmation as to the validity of the telegram, but I choose to believe it was authentic.

> *"The qualities of creativity and genius are within you, awaiting your decision to match up with the power of intention."*
> ~ Wayne Dyer

When we can control our creative energy, we start to enter the genius arena. We can try to access this creative state all we want, but our wanting and trying are fueled by our desire. Desire is our all-access backstage pass. The intensity of our desire strongly influences our ability to transmute energy from one form to another because the formless (strong thoughts of desire) has a frequency that acts as a magnet to attract the same frequency of its physical form (physical reality and real-life experiences).

Whether we are aware of desires or not, they still exist. They can even be a complete surprise to us! Sometimes desires I didn't even know I had would emerge through automatic writing, flowing from my pen during Gratitude Journaling.

For example, on October 22nd, 2012, I manifested, "Writing a Bestselling book is something I'm very proud of." As I wrote this, I thought, "Who am I to write a book?" But even amidst the self-doubt, deep inside of me I knew that it would indeed happen.

I didn't think about becoming an author again until eight months later when I received an out-of-the-blue message on Facebook inviting me to collaborate on a book. Almost one year after writing that hand-scribbled surprise intention in my journal, I had my first International Bestselling book!

After initially becoming recognized as one of the 21 authors for the book *Hot Mama in (High) Heels - Daily Tips To Rock Your World As A Woman*, I'm thrilled to report that I'm now an Eight Time #1 International Bestselling Author.

I share these stories to demonstrate why I believe wholeheartedly in Albert Einstein's quote: "Imagination is everything. It is the preview of life's coming attractions." It's also my hope that my stories will inspire you to look back on your own life, identify where you've already transmuted thoughts into physical reality, and serve as a reminder to supercharge your thoughts with desire.

As I lift my hand to gently close the cover of my computer, I'm left with an overwhelming sense of anticipation as I find myself anxiously awaiting (backstage, with my all-access pass) for YOUR coming attractions.

MICKEY STEWART

About Mickey Stewart: Born in Cape Breton, Canada, Mickey Stewart is a musician, coach, and author who has been a player and instructor of the snare drum and bodhrán for forty years. Responsible for heading up the drum program at Ardvreck School in Perthshire, Scotland since 2002, Mickey is in high demand to teach throughout the U.K. and North America.

Creator and founder of *BodhránExpert.com*, her YouTube videos have received more than two million views from students and fans from every country throughout the world.

Over the past eight years, she's been involved in the TV and film industry as a supporting artist. Even more recently, she's begun following her newest passion, which is teaching others how to share their talents with the world.

Stewart lives in Crieff, Scotland with her husband of twenty-six years, Scottish musician and composer Mark Stewart, along with their 18-year-old son, Cameron, who is also a piper.

Author's Website: *www.MickeyStewart.com*

Book Series Website & Author's Bio: *www.The13StepsToRiches.com*

Natalie Susi

EVERYTHING IS ENERGY

Money is just energy. Everything is just energy. Energy is responsible for all of creation all of the time. We are all made up of these things called "atoms." Atoms are made up of 99 percent energy and 1 percent matter. For some reason, we have gotten stuck talking about the matter instead of the energy, and we've placed much more importance on the matter over the energy. This is the wrong part of the equation to focus on.

So, now let's get it right; let's talk about energy. Let's talk about transmutation. Transmutation is the alchemical process of changing or transforming one form of energy into another. Transmutation is the act of utilizing energy to create exactly what we desire.

If we can learn how this works and implement this into our daily lives, we can, at any moment, utilize energy to tap into our zone of genius, get aligned with the universe, and create the reality that we would love to experience in our lives.

In *Think and Grow Rich*, Napoleon Hill introduces a concept called "mind stimulants." He explains that these can act as vehicles to help us tap into our creative power and zone of genius. There are 10 mind stimulants: Eight of them are healthy, and they include the desire for self expression, love, money, music, friendship, mastermind alliance, mutual suffering, and auto-suggestion. Two of them are unhealthy, and they include fear and narcotics/alcohol.

When the healthy stimulants are harnessed and transmuted, they can empower people to step into their greatest visions of themselves, creating a domino effect of positive momentum that can propel someone to the next level of success. When we choose to engage in negative stimulants, we create destruction and chaos. We are still harnessing energy, but it is the kind of energy that erupts into destructive circumstances.

While I do not partake in any narcotics, and I do not overuse alcohol, I have gotten stuck in a perpetual cycle of negativity, engaging in the mind stimulant of fear. In my first business in the food and beverage industry, I was out of alignment with my purpose, so not surprisingly, I wasn't making any money.

I was constantly in a state of fear-based thinking, worst-case scenario thoughts, and glass-is-half-empty expectations about the outcomes of the business. The negative energy was translating into negative results.

As a result, I was creating a space for nonsense to ensue in my life and business. I was in such a fear cycle that I rarely engaged in the positive mind stimulants, so I felt like I was either running in place or taking five steps forward and ten steps back. I didn't feel like I could gain any kind of significant momentum. I spent a ton of time feeling stuck and very little time feeling successful.

Our mind is so powerful. As Tony Robbins says, "Where focus goes, energy flows." What we think about, we bring about. It is our choice to choose healthy mind stimulants or unhealthy ones. It is a simple decision but not always an easy one.

On the other side of that coin, I always utilize healthy stimulants in my current business as a coach, consultant, and professor. And as a result, I align with my purpose, my business is totally in flow, and I produce great results for my clients and make an abundant living doing so.

I attract soul clients seeking and wanting to work with me. I do not have to cold call, chase, or persuade clients to pay me the rate that I am asking. I am clear about my value and worth; my clients are too. I never feel like I am on a treadmill running in place and wasting precious time and energy. I can also feel the momentum of success that continues to build. I can tap into my creativity and intuitive abilities, and I feel like I am working with infinite intelligence to receive downloads, ideas, and insights that I can use to help my clients.

There is a stark contrast between the energetic space that I was living in as a business owner who was engaging in unhealthy mind stimulants and the energetic space I live in now as an entrepreneur engaged in healthy mind stimulants.

Positive mind stimulants have an energetic domino effect. They ignite momentum and increase the vibration of your mind, leading to the heightened creative imagination that allows you to tap into your sixth sense or your intuitive abilities.

Creative imagination is the direct link between the finite human mind and infinite intelligence. All discoveries occur through the faculty of creative imagination. It functions best when the mind is vibrating due to one of the mind stimulants at an exceedingly high rate.

The best way to utilize this process to create, solve problems, and develop new ideas is to first stimulate your mind through one of these stimulants and, second, concentrate on what your creation looks and sounds and feels like when it's done. Take a deep breath. Free your mind of any worries or low vibrational thoughts. Allow these to flow out and replace them with high-vibrational thoughts and images. Create a clear picture. This can lead you to your highest genius. Hold the picture in your mind until it is taken over by your subconscious, and then relax, clear your head of all thoughts, and wait for the answer to flash in your mind.

I encourage you to take the time today to reflect on your desires. Write down the positive mind stimulants you are engaging in, and then write down any negative ones. Commit to releasing fear-based thoughts and actions and any misuse or overuse of alcohol and narcotics.

Write down your intention to release the negative ones and step into the positive ones. Write down your mission, vision, goals, and/or the desires that you want to call into your existence now. Write down your WHY for why they matter in your life and why you're compelled to create a reality that includes them.

Make sure you are clear about WHY you want to create this reality. The more committed and engaged you are about your why, the easier it will be to align with the positive mind stimulants over the negative ones and utilize the energy to attract your desires most efficiently and effectively.

Transmutation is the most powerful force for calling in your desires now. It will lift the mind to the status of a genius. It will connect you to your inner voice, your intuition, and the universe's infinite intelligence. It will transcend time and space and physically attract what you desire, like magic. It will allow you to create endless possibilities and draw you closer to your purpose and desires more than anything else on this planet.

NATALIE SUSI

About Natalie Susi: Natalie has more than 14 years of experience as a teacher, speaker, entrepreneur and mentor. Currently she's a 5-year UCSD professor focusing on communications and the Pursuit of Happiness. As an entrepreneur, she founded and grew Bare Organic Mixers beverage company for 8 years resulting in an acquisition in 2014.

After selling the company, Natalie combined her educational background as a teacher and her experience as an entrepreneur to provide personal development coaching and consulting to individuals, businesses, and creative entrepreneurs. She develop a program called Conscious Conversations and utilizes a step-by-step process called The Alignment Method to support leaders in cultivating conscious teams and businesses through a process of self-reflection, self-discover, and self-ascension that ultimately increases profits, productivity, and the growth of the individuals, personally and professionally.

Author's Website: *www.NatalieSusi.com*

Book Series Website & Author's Bio: *www.The13StepsToRiches.com*

Nita Patel

TRANSMUTATION ENERGY

Ask yourself, "What am I obsessing over?" Where do you spend most of your energy? It evolves over time but keep your awareness on where your obsession lies on a regular basis. Is it watching Netflix? TikToks? Instagram Reels? Or are you so concerned about the news that you get every news feed about all the worldly events daily? Are you concerned about being lonely and make continuous poor choices in the people you surround yourself with? Or do you block out the world and act like your job is the only thing keeping you alive?

The truth is all these things are *killing you softly.* They are robbing you of your creative and resourceful energy—that is, if you're interested in living a fulfilled, purpose-driven and wealthy life. We are talking about a key step to riches here, so let's be open about how any addiction is robbing you from living your best life.

How do you live your best life? With balance. That means no single area of your life is suffering because you're fulfilled in all areas of your life: You have financial security, health, connectedness and healthy relationships; you practice self-care often, and have spirituality, hobbies, and a career that brings you joy.

Yes, the focus of this conversation is about steps to riches, but money alone is not a step to riches. Ask someone who has money but lacks healthy relationships—there is no true peace or joy with one area of your life out of balance.

Transmutation is all about taking the obsessive energy that is wasting your time and channeling it into fueling your purpose, passion and something that is fulfilling to you. It's that creative force that you may not think you have, but trust me, you absolutely do, and you can direct it to build something for yourself or to support someone who is aligned with your values.

It can be as simple as focusing on your health and playing tennis with a group of people every week to finding a new passion and turning it into a career. It can be ways of contributing to the community and world at large, while simultaneously giving you financial freedom.

When you sit in front of your TV or iPad or Phone to watch reels, or to binge watch a show, how much time passes before you realized it's 4 hours past your bedtime? Sometimes you even get a reminder on the screen to take a break or it will ask if you are still watching. Rather than being sucked into the world of someone else's life, take that time to rest, wake up early and work out.

Yes, I said work out, first thing in the morning. It is scientifically proven that when you work out first thing in the morning, your blood sugar is regulated, your brain functions better, you have mental clarity to make sound decisions, and even if you sneak in a chocolate croissant for breakfast, your body can process it without worrying about it going to your heart, hips or wherever your body likes to store the "good stuff" that's not so good for you.

Being healthy is the most important step to riches because it impacts your brain health far more than you know. John Ratey and Eric Hageman discuss research in their book *Spark,* that was done in the Naperville, Illinois school district.

They took a group of elementary kids and had them exercise earlier in the day. This was not a traditional PE class that we're all too familiar with: The kids would do any form of movement which elevated their heart rate for a particular amount of time. The kids who liked to dance, danced; those who enjoyed sports played sports. They were allowed to be creative with any activity that created movement in the body. These kids were given their math and science tests right after their exercise class.

The results showed that the kids who exercised right before they took a test scored significantly higher than those who did not participate in the exercise. Even if they exercised later in the afternoon, there was no significant impact to test scores. This research shows that morning exercise keeps our brain sharp. If you're in school and have finals coming up, it's that much more important to get your work out in. For the rest of you who need support in daily decision making, especially if you're here to live your best life, this is critical for you.

Channeling your energy, time, thoughts and head space to that which is going to allow you to live your best life is key to your success. Journaling and meditating are very important to keeping inventory of where your time and energy are spent. Practice both as time permits to hold yourself accountable.

Napolean Hill had a famous line he shared about how once the riches start coming in, it's a snowball effect and you'll wonder where it's been this whole time. Isn't that the part we're all waiting for, that infamous snowball effect? Keep this inventory step in mind as you journey to your snowball effect moment.

There are many online assessments you can find to get a good feel for how balanced or imbalanced your life is. Find the courage to know your truth. It's all the little steps that take you to the top of the mountain. If your mountain is being a published author, it's seeing a physical copy of your book in your hands.

If your mountain is receiving an Emmy or Oscar, it's holding the award in your hands. If your mountain is to be a philanthropist, it's seeing how many lives you've impacted through your work. We all have very different mountain tops we're reaching for, as we should. Be bold and brave in your calling and pursue it one step at a time. This is your key to success.

NITA PATEL

About Nita Patel: Nita is a Bestselling Author, speaker, and artist who believes in modern etiquette as a path to becoming our best selves.

Through her professional years, Ms. Patel has 25 years of demonstrated technology leadership experience in various industries specifically with a concentrated focus in health care for 14 of those 20+ years. She's shown her art across the world to include the Louvre in Paris. She's a Bestselling Author and performance coach, pursuing her master's in industrial organizational (I-O) psychology at Harvard. Her investment in psychology theory and practice is what led her to a deep interest in helping others. She has become deeply and passionately devoted to nurturing others and in building their confidence and brand through speaking and consultative practices.

Author's Website: *www.Nita-Patel.com*

Book Series Website & Author's Bio: *www.The13StepsToRiches.com*

Olga Geidane

WITH DELIBERATION, PURPOSE, AND FORETHOUGHT

"A relatively small number of people use WITH DELIBERATION, PURPOSE, AND FORETHOUGHT the faculty of Creative Imagination. Those who use this faculty voluntarily and with understanding of its functions are, by definition, geniuses."
~ Napoleon Hill

OLGA GEIDANE

About Olga Geidane: Olga is an International Speaker, an Event MC/Host, Facilitator, Mindset Coach, a Bestselling Author, and a Regional President of the Professional Speaking Association in the UK. She is a host of Olga's Show and A World-Traveler.

Olga helps ambitious people to unlock their extraordinary performance and their true, authentic side. She is passionate about helping people to live their best lives. Olga knows how tough it is to be broke and unfulfilled in life: at the age of 24, just after her divorce, Olga came to the UK from Latvia with no spoken English, with just £100 in her pocket, and a 2.5-year-old son. Olga is a very inspirational survivor: she went through abuse, betrayal, cheating, financial loss, and emotional breakdown. Matt Black (Business Model Innovation & Disruption Consultant—Snr. Advisor to CEO CSO CCO COO—Author & International Public Speaker) said: "Olga really takes it up a notch beyond anything I have seen before. She is one of the bravest people I have ever seen on stage. If you are looking to book a speaker or attend a talk that will be inspiring, challenging, and leave you wanting to take action... She is perfect."

Author's Website: *www.OlgaGeidane.com*

Book Series Website & Author's Bio: *www.The13StepsToRiches.com*

Paul Capozio

THE ROAD TO GENIUS

"There is no other road to genius than through voluntary self-effort!"
~ Napoleon Hill

PAUL CAPOZIO

About Paul Capozio: Paul Capozio was born in Hoboken, New Jersey, and grew up on the streets of Hudson County. At 35, he was recruited to be the President of Sales and Marketing for a 350-million-dollar human resources firm. In 7 years, he drove the top-line revenue of that firm to over 1.5 billion.

Capozio owns and operates Capco Capital, Inc., an investment and consulting firm. The majority of Capco's holdings are of manufacturers and distributors of health and wellness products and human resources firms. Capco provides sales consulting and training, helping companies increase sales through traditional and direct sales disciplines. Making the invisible visible and simplifying the complex is his stock and trade.

A dynamic public speaker, he provides motivation and "meat and potatoes" skills to those in the health and wellness field who do not consider themselves "salespeople," allowing their voices to be heard above the "noise."

He is a husband of 32 years to his wife, Linda. He is also a father and grandfather.

Author's Website: *www.PaulCapozio.com*

Purchase Book Online: *www.The13StepsToRiches.com*

Phillip McClure

THE IMPORTANCE OF FOCUSING ON YOUR GOALS

The Perils of Love

Every "hi" is a potential "bye" to your success. Every interaction with someone to whom you are attracted, whether it's just a friendly conversation or a full-blown flirtation, has the potential to distract us from our goals. While it's important to have social interactions and build relationships, we must also be mindful of the impact they have on our focus and productivity.

We live in a world where physical attraction energy plays a significant role in our social lives. It's natural to be drawn to someone who appears to be beautiful, and we may feel a sense of excitement or curiosity when we see such a person.

However, sometimes this attraction can lead us down a path that may not be in our best interest. Seeing an attractive person and ignoring or avoiding them is a situation that many of us may have experienced in our lives. It can be tempting to get caught up in the allure of love and relationships, but it's important to remember that every moment and every dollar spent on a potential partner could be slowing down your wealth creation and destroying your ability to invest in opportunities.

Before we delve into the topic of avoiding attractive people, it's essential to discuss the importance of becoming a person of value and focus. This means focusing on developing yourself, your skills, and your passions, rather than solely pursuing someone of interest.

When you become a person of value, you attract other valuable people into your life, including potential partners. Becoming a person of value should be a priority before even considering becoming a probable suitor. You need to have something to offer beyond your physical appearance or fleeting charm.

When you focus on building your skills, knowledge, and personal brand, you become more attractive to potential partners who are looking for a long-term commitment. It's easy to get caught up in the excitement of a new relationship, but it's important to remember that using attraction energy towards a limited time goal or gratification can slow down your progress towards achieving your goals. It's important to remain focused on your goals and not let your emotions cloud your judgment.

It's essential to prioritize your goals and work towards them with dedication and focus. Every minute and dollar you spend pursuing love takes away from your ability to invest in yourself and create opportunities for wealth creation. When you become successful, you naturally attract people who share your values and are interested in your journey.

Love can be dangerous; love is a very powerful emotion that can have significant consequences if not managed appropriately. When you are in the throes of love, it's easy to lose sight of your goals and become overly focused on the person you are interested in. This can lead to a lack of focus and a decrease in productivity, which can ultimately hurt your chances of success.

Love, because it is such a powerful emotion, can cloud your judgment and lead you down a path that you may later regret. It's important to be aware of the emotional highs that can rob you of your success-minded thinking and create dopamine that overtakes your true happiness. The pursuit of love can be a distraction from achieving your goals and can lead to poor financial decisions.

When you focus on building your wealth and investing in your future, you create a foundation for long-term success that can sustain you even if your romantic relationships falter.

How do you deal with the emotional highs that come with falling in love? How do you maintain a focus on your goals and avoid the pitfalls that can come with being in a relationship? If you find that you are in a relationship that is interfering with your goals or that is not healthy for you, it may be time to consider ending it. This can be a difficult decision, but it's important to remember that your long-term success and happiness should be your top priority.

In some cases, it may be necessary to seek professional help to deal with the emotional highs of love and to ensure that you are making decisions that are in line with your goals. A therapist or coach can help you to identify your priorities and develop strategies for achieving them.

Become aware of the emotional highs that can accompany love. It's important to recognize that these feelings are not necessarily indicative of a healthy relationship. You need to be able to separate your emotions from your goals and make rational decisions based on your long-term objectives.

It's also important to set boundaries and prioritize your own needs. It's easy to get caught up in the needs of a partner and forget about your own. Remember that you are the only person who can truly look out for your best interests.

Transmutative energy is a powerful force that can drive us towards our goals, but it can also be a destructive force when not used wisely. When you use transmutative energy towards a limited time goal or gratification, you place yourself in a tar that slows down your body and mind from achieving your true potential. When we let our desires take over, we place ourselves in a position that slows us down from achieving our goals.

Transmutative energy is a powerful force that can be harnessed for positive results. However, when we use it for short-term gratification, we risk losing sight of our long-term objectives.

It's crucial to recognize the potential dangers of pursuing someone solely based on physical attraction. While it may bring temporary pleasure, it can ultimately lead to disappointment and a lack of fulfillment. Instead, focus on building meaningful relationships with people who share your values and are interested in supporting your goals.

Dealing with Emotional Highs

When you experience emotional highs, it's important to recognize them for what they are and not let them distract you from your goals. Dopamine, a neurotransmitter that plays a significant role in pleasure and motivation, can be released when you experience feelings of love and attraction.

However, it's essential to recognize that these feelings are temporary and to not let them cloud your judgment. To deal with emotional highs, it's important to focus on your long-term goals and prioritize your actions accordingly. Recognize that temporary pleasure is not worth sacrificing your future success and happiness. If you find yourself becoming overly focused on a particular person or emotion, take a step back and evaluate your priorities.

Love is a powerful emotion that can be dangerous when it distracts us from our goals. When we fall in love, we experience a rush of dopamine and euphoria that can be addictive. We become so consumed with our feelings that we lose sight of our priorities and goals. This can lead to poor decision-making and lack of focus, which can harm our chances of success.

The emotional highs that love creates can overtake our success-minded thinking of true happiness. We must learn to deal with our emotions effectively and not let them cloud our judgment. It's important to recognize the moments when our emotions are taking over and practice self-control. This means understanding our triggers, avoiding situations that may lead to temptation, and learning to let go of negative feelings.

To deal with the dangers of love, we must have a clear understanding of our values, goals, and priorities. We must know what we want and be willing to make the necessary sacrifices to achieve it. We must also be willing to accept that sometimes, the best course of action is to walk away from a situation that is not serving our best interests.

In conclusion, ignoring or avoiding a beautiful woman is not about being antisocial or neglecting our social needs. It's about being mindful of our priorities and goals and ensuring that our actions align with them. It's about becoming a person of value, harnessing our transmutative energy for positive results, and learning to deal with our emotions effectively. By doing so, we can achieve true happiness and fulfillment in both our personal and professional lives.

While love and relationships can be fulfilling, it's important to remember that they can also be a distraction from achieving your goals. It's important to focus on becoming a person of value, setting boundaries, and prioritizing your own needs.

By maintaining a focus on your long-term objectives and making rational decisions based on your goals, you can create a foundation for long-term success and happiness that will sustain you even if your strongest relationships falter.

PHILLIP MCCLURE

About Phillip D. McClure: Phillip is married to the love of his life, Maaike McClure, and is a very proud father of two exciting kids. He was raised in the great state of Montana before moving to Utah. Phil lives life to the fullest. His accomplishments consist of completing a full Ironman, and deploying four times with the Army, earning multiple decorations along the way—including two Utah crosses! This makes him the only soldier in history to receive that medal twice.

Currently, Phil is the Owner of NorthStar Coins, Events by NorthStar, the co-owner of P.B. Fast Cars, and recruits pilots for the Army Aviation program. It was during his last deployment that he accidentally created his first Mastermind and it has forever changed his life as well as the others involved. He mentors and coaches in self-improvement and physical fitness.

Phil is an exotic car enthusiast that spends as much time behind the wheel as possible, whether it is carving through canyons, ripping around the racetrack, or coaching others to see their potential. Competitive driving is the best therapy in the world.

Live life to the fullest and have fun while doing it. You don't get a rewind in life so take mistakes as the lessons they are and improve, but don't make the same mistakes twice. Live in flow, not with the flow.

Authors website: *www.NorthStarCoins.com*

Book Series Website: *www.The13StepsToRiches.com*

Robyn Scott

YOUR UNICORN FACTOR

"The world is ruled, and the destiny of civilization is established, by human emotions. People are influenced by their actions, not by reason but by 'feelings.' The creative faculty of the mind is set into action entirely by emotions, and not by cold reason."
~ Napoleon Hill

The world is engulfed with billions of people having hundreds of emotions all the time. Many individuals are subservient victims of their emotions. I know Hill is talking more about those of us who have mastered our emotions!

Once we understand the root of the emotions we are feeling, we then, and only then, can respond to those emotions rather than reacting to them. So, how do we master our emotions?

According to Napolean Hill, "The emotions are states of mind. Nature has provided man with a 'chemistry of the mind' which operates in a manner similar to the principles of chemistry of matter." Our minds are having a chemical reaction; we can feel that. This is our warning signal.

With practice and effort, we can intentionally pause and observe the emotion we feel in our bodies. Hill refers to this as voluntary self-effort: "There is no other road to genius than through voluntary self-effort!"

I'll share my example of anger. I was a slave to it, constantly apologizing for my raging outbursts as they bubbled over and spewed out all over the people around me. To understand and change how anger looked at me, I had to learn what anger truly represents. Anger is simply amped-up sadness. Yep, that's it! If I could look within myself and find that sadness, I could address it.

Hill teaches us to "Encourage the presence of these emotions as the dominating thoughts in one's mind, and discourage the presence of all the destructive emotions. The mind is a creature of habit. It thrives upon the dominating thoughts fed to it. Through the faculty of willpower, one may discourage the presence of any emotion and encourage the presence of any other. Control of the mind through the power of will is not difficult. Control comes from persistence and habit. The secret of control lies in understanding the process of transmutation. When any negative emotion presents itself in one's mind, it can be transmuted into a positive or constructive emotion by changing one's thoughts." In short, perspective means everything.

This means that if I keep doing what I am doing, nothing will change. However, we have the choice of intention and reasoning regarding our emotions. Napoleon Hill said, "I encourage you to look at your negative emotions and truly discern where they originated from." You can master yourself! Napoleon Hill knew it, and I do, too! I believe in you!

We all experience emotions. We do not experience them like anyone else, past, present, or future. You are here with your divine perspectives, which is important to realize. You can come from the same family, place, family make-up as, say your siblings, but you each have unique perspectives! I want you to know YOUR perspective; how you look at things and experience emotion is 100% all yours! As we continue through this chapter, keep that in mind.

"The human mind responds to stimulation...a mind stimulant is any influence which will either temporarily, or permanently, increase the vibrations of thought." Additionally, Hill teaches that the "stimuli to which the mind responds most freely are the desire for self expression, love, a burning desire for fame, power, or financial gain and MONEY, music, a friendship between either those of the same sex or those of the opposite sex, a Master Mind alliance based upon the harmony of two or more people who ally themselves for spiritual or temporal advancement, mutual suffering, such as that experienced by people who are persecuted, auto-suggestion, fear, and narcotics and alcohol."

Here is a concept I have been practicing, and it has helped a lot during the dark times when our vibration is so low we feel we cannot raise it. You can be your own high. Gratitude is an undermined shortcut to raise your vibration. Gratitude has the energy of raw love. The simplest and most powerful way to raise your vibration is to return to being thankful —even if it is just for the shoes on your feet or a toothbrush.

I encourage you to practice gratitude often and consistently. Saying it out loud and writing it down deepens the energy in your body and mind. We all deserve to be in a high vibration within ourselves. It is our divine right to feel good, enough, worthy, and loved. It's simple, I know, and it works!

As we continue going over the transmutation of energy, if you feel negative thoughts or old beliefs coming to mind, remember to be grateful for anything! Be a "silver-lininger" as we have some fun diving into getting what we desire through our inspiration!

Hill taught, "When ideas or concepts flash into one's mind, through what is popularly called a "hunch," they come from one or more of the following sources:

1. Infinite Intelligence

2. One's subconscious mind wherein is stored every sense impression and thought impulse which ever reached the brain through any of the five senses

3. From the mind of some other person who has just released the thought or picture of the idea or concept through conscious thought, or

4. From the other person's subconscious storehouse.

When we are in a spot where we can be at peace (and there are infinite ways to get there), we are in a receiving place to be inspired. We all have this within us. No one is excluded from receiving from one of these four sources. In personal development, some refer to these as "downloads." I did not know this. I truly believed I was not able or deserved to receive inspiration. I am very grateful I know better now.

Find your own way to peace. Meditation, yoga, prayer, etc., whatever works for you is perfect for YOU! It is important that your mind is "stilled." Our minds, having only a finite limitation, need to be free of distraction to receive and hear our own downloads. The world is loud and can be overbearing. This practice helps us also keep our vibrations up.

There are dozens of ways to doubt ourselves, and I am here to tell you the world needs YOUR DOWNLOADS! YOUR CONCEPTS! YOUR HUNCHES! YOU are the only one to receive them and share them with others. This is your Unicorn Factor! You are destined to be a part of this world right now, and only you can reach those who you were meant to inspire and assist as we travel through this life journey. Einstein was here for a reason, exactly when he was supposed to be. You may not invent as he did, and it makes your insights nothing short of its own genius!

A better definition of a genius "is a man who has discovered how to increase the vibrations of thought to the point where he can freely communicate with sources of knowledge not available through the ordinary rate of vibration of thought."

Hill talks about how most successful people are truly the MOST successful after age 50! I just turned 50 and want to share my thoughts on why he talks about it at length. I have very little time or energy to care what others think of me. It is draining and so harmful to our good vibrations!

At some point, we have to not care—we have to not care how others perceive us, not care what we look like compared to others. We may have to not care if we are disappointing people who have no concept of themselves and do not care who is judging us. Let all other opinions roll off your back if it is negative or hurtful.

YOU KNOW who you are deep down. You KNOW what is best for you, and you KNOW you are here for a divine purpose. Feedback is always welcome, of course. Apply it if you desire, and never feel like you have to. This, to me, is wisdom! And yes, it does come with age. I see it sooner and sooner in people now, and I am so thrilled I can see it in me.

Above all, be enthusiastic in all you do! Hill teaches us how important that is in chapter 11 as well! With enough enthusiasm for your desire, you really can transmute the energy to get what you want!

ROBYN SCOTT

About Robyn Scott: Scott is a Habit Finder Coach and has worked closely with the president, Paul Blanchard, at the Og Mandino Group. She is also a certified Master Your Emotions Coach through Inscape World. Robyn Scott is commonly known in professional communities as the Queen of Connection and Princess of Play. She has been working hard for the past nine years to hone her skills as a mentor and coach. Scott strives to teach people to annihilate judgments, embrace their own stories, and empower themselves to rediscover who they truly are. Scott is an international speaker and also teaches how to present yourself on stage.

Her first book, *Bringing People Together: Rediscovering the Lost Art of Face-to-Face Connecting, Collaborating, and Creating* was released in August 2019 and was a bestseller in seven categories.

Author's Website: *www.RobynKayeScott.com*

Book Series Website & Author's Bio: *www.The13StepsToRiches.com*

Shannon Whittington

CHANGE IS THE ONLY TRUE CONSTANT

If you want to be successful, no matter your goal, you must first open yourself to the concept of transmutation. It's been said that change is the only true constant; it happens every second of every day, from the smallest atom to entire galaxies and beyond. Taking your life to the next level means having the will and the courage to determine what you want to change about yourself and making a plan accordingly.

To help you on this journey, here are a few ways to help you transmute into the person you're destined to become.

Determine your Goal

Change is inevitable, but we can decide who we will become. This is why it's so important to ask yourself: Who do I want to be? Where do I see myself in a year or five to ten years from now? What kind of job do I want? How am I going to get to where I'm going? These questions are the building blocks to transmutation and will help you determine your destiny.

Once you have the answers to these questions, even if it's only a few answers, it becomes so much easier to fulfill them because you now have a road map to your own personal success.

For example, I've known ever since I was a kid that I wanted to become a nurse because I wanted to help people. As I got older, I asked myself, "If this is who I want to be, how will I get there?" I made a plan to go to school, and I put every ounce of effort into my education. Once I graduated, I knew I didn't want to stop there, so I continued my transmutation by setting a goal of finishing graduate school.

I saw how far along my peers were than me, and I knew I wanted to be the go-to person for LGBTQ+ health, so I focused on getting even more education. Today, I'm giving speeches and providing knowledge and insight to many healthcare professionals because I had a simple goal as a child and the desire to help others.

Embrace Discomfort

Transmutation and our comfort zones do not mix. If we want to achieve true success, we must absolutely be willing to be uncomfortable. It's easy to remain stagnant in our careers and in our lives. When things are going "just fine," there is a strong temptation to not make any sudden movements out of fear of shaking our foundation. But I'm here to tell you that only when you embrace discomfort will you become who you're destined to be.

Let's say that you want a promotion at your job. You may have to take on extra tasks, work overtime, or maybe even go back to school to get the promotion. As I mentioned earlier, I went back to school over and over again, and in doing so, I pushed my way out of my comfort zone. I knew that the discomfort of difficult coursework, intense studying, and little to no free time would be worth it in the long run, and I never lost sight of my goals.

To achieve yours, you cannot be happy sitting still; you must focus on where you want to be and never lose sight, especially when things are difficult.

Watch your Thoughts

There is a quote attributed to Lao Tzu that I hold close to my heart: "Watch your thoughts, they become your words; watch your words, they become your actions; watch your actions, they become your habits; watch your habits, they become your character; watch your character, it becomes your destiny."

The person you are destined to become stems from even the tiniest thoughts that percolate in your head. Embracing transmutation means being mindful of these thoughts, so they do not derail you from achieving your goals.

For instance, it's easy to think negative thoughts when doing work we don't want to do. When we're in the thick of it, whether it's a particularly challenging homework assignment or a work task that just doesn't seem to end, our thoughts can drift into negative territory. "I can put this task off for a while before it's due;" "I just don't see the point in any of this;" "Maybe I should just quit while I'm ahead."

By recognizing these thoughts for what they are, you give yourself the strength to push them aside and change them into positive ones: "Look at how far I've come along;" "I'm going to feel so much better to get this done;" "This is a building block to my personal success." Thoughts matter and you have the power to counteract them when necessary.

Learn from your Mistakes

Another quote that speaks volumes to me is by James Joyce: "A [person's] errors are [their] portals of discovery." I can't even begin to tell you about all the mistakes I've made on the road to success, and I'm thankful for every last one of them. They have not only taught me what I shouldn't do, but they've also given me incredible insights into who I am as an individual. My mistakes have highlighted areas of my life, whether personal or professional, that need fine-tuning so that I don't make those same mistakes in the future.

However, when we acknowledge our mistakes, it can become easy for many of us to ruminate, dwell, and guilt ourselves for committing them in the first place. This leads to absolutely nowhere useful.

When you look back at your past mistakes, consider how far you've come since making them. Think of all the little and not-so-little successes you've achieved. Think about how much you've learned and all the wisdom you can impart to others on their journeys. Think about how little your mistakes ultimately matter and how they never stopped you from working toward your destiny.

Collaborate with and Learn from Peers

I will always reiterate how important it is to not isolate yourself, including when it comes to transmuting into the person you're destined to be. In our society, so much emphasis is put on rugged individualism when the reality is that every successful person has relied on at least one other person to get where they are today.

I can't encourage you enough, no matter how much of an individualist you may pride yourself on being, to reach out and learn from and collaborate with others.

When I was pursuing my doctorate, there were days when I felt completely overwhelmed and unsure if I could achieve it at all. However, a thought occurred to me: I can't possibly be the only one in my class feeling this way. So, I emailed all seven people in my class, explaining how nervous and overwhelmed I was and that I suspected I wasn't the only one. I proposed that we start a text group to keep each other accountable and also offer support and advice as needed. Everyone in my class sent me a response saying they felt the exact same way.

At that moment, seven isolated and afraid students transmuted into what we would later dub "the magnificent seven." We only had one rule among us: You can whine and wine, but you cannot quit. And because of our scrappy collaboration, all seven of us walked across the stage at graduation with smiles on our faces.

As I mentioned, transmutation is almost never easy. It requires constant vigilance of your thoughts, careful and attentive planning for the future, an embracement of discomfort, insight into your past, and the willingness to reach out when you're feeling overwhelmed. It may be difficult, but it will lead you to wherever you want to go, and it all starts with one simple thought: "I am ready to change."

SHANNON WHITTINGTON

About Dr. Shannon Whittington: Shannon (she/her) is a speaker, author, consultant, and clinical nurse educator. Her area of expertise is LGBTQ+ inclusion in the workplace. Whittington has a passion for transgender health where she educates clinicians in how to care for transgender individuals after undergoing gender-affirming surgeries.

Whittington was honored to receive the Quality and Innovation Award from the Home Care Association of New York for her work with the transgender population. She was recently awarded the Notable LGBTQ+ Leaders & Executives award by Crain's New York Business, Daisy Award for Outstanding Nurses, as well as the International Association of Professionals Nurse of the Year award. Whittington is a city and state lobbyist for transgender equality.

To date, Whittington has presented virtually and in person at various organizations and conferences across the nation, delivering extremely well-received presentations. Her forthcoming books include *LGBTQ+: ABC's For Grownups* and *Kindergarten for Leaders: 9 Essential Tips For Grownup Success.*

Author's Website: *www.linkedin.com/in/ShannonWhittington*

Book Series Website & Author's Bio: *www.The13StepsToRiches.com*

Soraiya Vasanji

YOUR ENERGY MATTERS

What does your name mean? Did you grow up knowing the meaning and wonder why this name was chosen for you? Amidst all the fun, interesting, and meaningful names, how did the universe support your family in choosing this name for you?

Well, I did wonder! My name—Soraiya—has an Arabic origin, and it means precious gem, like the highly-coveted stones such as diamonds, rubies, and sapphires. I love the meaning of my name. Yet, I have always had an intuitive sense that there was a greater depth to why I received this name. These precious gemstones undergo great heat and pressure to transform mud and minerals into spectacular, valuable rocks. This type of transformation is a kind of transmutation.

Transmutation is transferring one set of materials with low value into a new set of materials with high value. It is more than a coincidence that many strangers I meet—in restaurants, airplanes, Pilates classes, and checkout lines—all ask if they know me from somewhere. "I have that face!" I usually say.

However, the truth I have embraced is that they are attracted to my light; their vibration is meeting my high vibration, creating a resonance of warmth and connection that washes over them, giving them this feeling of familiarity. Although we have never met before. This may sound too woo-woo on the surface, but upon looking deeper, what's happening is the transmutation of the energy of meeting into radical light and love that emanates from within.

People are attracted to my light, which fuels the light inside me to burn brighter. This light doesn't happen by the flick of a switch but rather by transmuting difficult scenarios into possibilities that no one could have imagined. My name reminds me of this quote:

> *"Grapes must be crushed to make wine*
> *Diamonds form under pressure*
> *Olives are pressed to release oil*
> *Seeds grow in darkness*
> *Whenever you feel crushed, under pressure, pressed, or in darkness,*
> *you're in a powerful place of transformation/transmutation."*
> ~ Lalah Delia

What is transmutation?

In simple terms, transmutation is the transferring of energy from one state into another state. In its simplest form, transmutation can be seen as changing one's circumstances so that you recognize you have the power of choice to change your situation. Then you take action, get out of your own way, and do it. You transmute a negative into a positive.

In essence, this is what happens in empowerment coaching. We look at the circumstances and realize that we may have been stuck seeing only one unfavorable solution when we should, instead, dive deeper into the mess and realize there are endless solutions when we harness the negative energy in a positive way. It always comes back to mindset.

While I rarely talk about this process of transmutation, it is happening all around us constantly. We are either transmuting or staying stuck. People often get stuck thinking the word positive means only happy and nice things, but that's not what I mean when I say a positive mindset.

Positivity, in this sense, means being open and capable of receiving and thinking in a higher sense. It means transcending the victimhood and low energy of the negative into possibility. It's not just shouting out affirmations and hoping everything will turn out okay. There is real neuroscience behind how we speak to ourselves, align ourselves with our purpose, and set intentions that play out in our subconscious and consciousness.

We are creating from our thoughts, so this is how we transmute our circumstances. It's possible, as humans, to create anything, and transmutation is the vehicle of creating something out of nothing or gaining something out of any situation, even one that looks desperate.

As Clive Barker, the author, playwright, and film director, summarizes, "Everything is in flux: everything changes; the body changes, the soul changes. We are capable of extraordinary self-transmutation and internal self-transformation."

A clear moment of transmutation is when one area of your life is in high vibration, where you are having success. You don't even know why, but you are so present in the moment of success that you don't realize how successful it is—you just fully trust it. This is how I felt during my second pregnancy, which led to the birth of our daughter, Naila.

I no longer thought in black and white; instead, similar to how I felt when applying to colleges, I thought of how it would feel to have a daughter and what our baby will be like. I stopped pushing and pulling and overanalyzing. Instead, I thought, in shades of colors, of how it would feel and what the baby would be like. I immersed myself in life-creating situations like being in nature, where birthing was happening all around me continuously.

I visited the ocean and transmuted the power of the waves into the power of creating life inside my own little uterine ocean. I had absolute certainty and shut everything out to be committed to this pregnancy—body, mind, and spirit. I surrounded myself with positive light and energy and a rhythmic, affirming belief that I would have a healthy pregnancy. It wasn't about me. It wasn't for me. It was about this soul out there coming forward and claiming their place in our family. Once I relaxed into this knowing and trusting, all pushing and pulling energy slipped away.

Many things in life that feel like they come naturally to us are really moments where transmutation energy is at play—creating something from another energetic state. I was vibrating high in my career, and I could pull that energy through into having a baby. I was in a different place of understanding, knowing, and trusting. I was in surrender. I was fully present in the current moment. I was vibrating at a different level.
How do we consciously replicate this? As an Energy Leadership Index Master Practitioner, I recognize that when we stop overanalyzing and start surrendering into our hearts, we drop from knowledge to wisdom.
This is when you can take knowledge and success from one area and transmute or apply that energy and vibration to a different area.

When we see transmutation as the transference of energy, the 7 levels of energy coined by Bruce Schneider become very clear. Here are the seven levels of energy and their respective scales of core thoughts, emotions, and resulting action. Level 1 is the lowest vibration, and level 7 is the highest frequency.

Level	Core Thought	Win Lose Game	Core Emotion	Feeling	Action
7	Non-Judgement	Winning and Losing are Illusions.	Absolute Passion	I am.	Creation
6	Synthesis	Everyone always wins.	Joy	I am you.	Wisdom
5	Reconciliation	We both win.	Peace	I understand you.	Acceptance
4	Concern	You win.	Compassion	I feel for you.	Service
3	Responsibility	I win.	Forgiveness	I forgive you.	Cooperation
2	Conflict	You lose.	Anger	I hate you.	Defiance
1	Victim	I lose.	Apathy	I hate myself.	Lethargy

When you meet someone and they say, "Whoa, do I know you from somewhere?" their energy is recognizing the high energy in you. Have you ever met someone and said to yourself, "Wowzah, I just got a hit of energy from that person"? Energy is transmuting from one person to another person. You received the energy, and it is now exciting for your own neurons to go off and fire.

Now you are in creation mode and formulating something that would never be until you received that transference spark. The transference of energy can happen physically and emotionally, like when you harness movement, and it fuels creativity.

The message behind transmutation is to BE INTENTIONAL IN YOUR LIFE. MAKE AND CREATE CHOICES. You are never stuck. You can take anything in a new direction at any time. It is your choice. They are all your choices. When you feel stuck, remember there is a possibility that you just haven't seen yet. When things feel like they are going in the wrong or different direction that you wish, take a pause and look at the scenario differently. It is your choice to choose a different pathway or trust the current pathway and know that there is something else to learn or see from this experience.

Also, think about what may be transmuting upon you and how to naturally bring about the forces of transmutation. Michio Kushi, a macrobiotic educator, shared the following:

"Peace begins in the kitchens and pantries, gardens, and backyards, where our food is grown and prepared. The energies of nature and the infinite universe are absorbed through the foods we eat and are transmuted into our thoughts and actions."

How does what you eat bring about changes to your thoughts and actions? Fuel your body with life-transforming properties. The saying "You are what you eat" is not that far off!

Step only in nature to experience the life force of the earth. I didn't fully understand the depth of what I was experiencing when I first started out with essential oils, but I now understand the impact of using doTERRA essential oils. When I roll Balance oil on the bottom of my feet, I feel the energy of deeply rooted Spruce trees. It's as if I am part of the root structure and can stand tall, feeling grounded and "balanced" to begin my day.

I transmute the energy of the land into my thoughts on how to empower and inspire others through my questions. When I breathe, these aromatic compounds in the olfactory system light up the brain stem. My hippocampus and amygdala are retrieving memories and simultaneously lighting up emotions like cheer, peace, and passion.

Along with these physical changes, my actions are changed. Similarly, when I apply lavender, vetiver, or Serenity to my palms and breathe in, I transmute the stillness and peace into my thoughts and actions. Actions are powerful, and it starts with our vibrating energy. Your energy matters.

SORAIYA VASANJI

About Soraiya Vasanji: Soraiya is a Certified Professional Coach (CPC), Energy Leadership Index Master Practitioner (ELI-MP), and has a Master's in Business Administration (MBA) from Kellogg University. She inspires women to be present, not perfect, ditch what doesn't serve them, and create their best messy life now. She loves sharing her wisdom on mindset, the power of language, self-love, self-worth, and leadership principles. She is the founder of the Mommy Mindset Summit series, and the Mom Mindset Reset Method coaching program. She empowers moms to move from tired, frustrated and depleted in their life to a creating the calm, happy and emotional even life for them and their families - no longer swinging from "energizer bunny mom" to dead on the couch!

Soraiya is married to her soulmate, has a young daughter, and lives in Toronto, Canada. She is a foodie, a jetsetter, a doTERRA essential oil enthusiast and she loves collecting unique crafting and stationery products!

Author's Website: *www.SoraiyaVasanji.com*

Book Series Website & Author's Bio: *www.The13StepsToRiches.com*

Stacey Ross Cohen

DESIRE AND TRANSMUTATION YIELDS SUCCESS

"The starting point of all achievement is desire."
~ Napoleon Hill

Napoleon Hill always emphasized that achieving wealth—or any other kind of success—doesn't occur by merely wishing for it. Success also requires action, tenacity, and mixing several other ingredients.

For example, desire mixed with transmutation propels us toward our goals. Understanding and applying this recipe is incredibly important for achieving success, and it's the subject of this chapter.

Desire is a powerful force when pursuing wealth, health, love, or anything else. But it needs a companion: transmutation. Just as a seed cannot grow into a tree without first going through the process of transmutation, our desires cannot materialize without undergoing a similar transformation. You can desire all you want, but if you don't take steps to make it happen, you'll never see your desires become a reality.

The Art and Science of Transmutation

Let's talk about science first. The law of the perpetual transmutation of energy is one of the most important laws in physics. It states that energy can neither be created nor destroyed—but can be transformed from one form to another. For example, when fossil fuel is burned, the chemical energy in the fuel is converted into heat and light. Water is another great example. It can transition into an ice cube, rain, or steam but never disappears entirely.

We can apply the law of transmutation to our lives by transforming our desire into what we want. We must focus on transmuting negative energy into positive energy to achieve more love, joy, and abundance in our lives. Fear, anger, and resentment can be turned into optimism, hope, and gratitude.

Transmuting this energy might entail taking concrete steps toward your goal, say, enrolling in a class or launching a business, or simply shifting your mindset to one of optimism using techniques like visualization and affirmations.

Born with Desire

While desire is not in your DNA, having parents who dream big is a major influence.

My parents (who are my biggest inspiration) had big dreams. Neither of them was college educated or had a leg up; my father lost his parents at age 17. But they were extremely driven to make a good life for us. My father worked in sales by day and played drums in a band at night; my mother was a full-time bookkeeper and often brought work home. By the time I turned nine, they had saved enough money to move from a small apartment in Brooklyn to a beautiful house in the suburbs.

My family was entrepreneurial. Both my parents launched successful businesses in fashion and real estate. I vividly recall my father sharing his new company name and logo, emblazoned on custom pencils.

Because of this, I've always been in search of challenges. I started my first home waitress service business at age 14 with my friend, Jen. Driven to make more than the standard hourly babysitting rate, we placed an ad in the local newspaper reading, "We Set, Serve & Clean up. Let us help you at your next party." We ended up increasing our earnings by 500%.

Having a successful business at a young age was one of my desires, but it wasn't my very first desire. That distinction? My desire was to cultivate a unique identity. Let me explain: I'm a twin. And as a twin, it's challenging to become your own person when there's someone just a few feet away who looks similar. My sister Shari and I shared toys, clothes, bedrooms, friends, and love from our parents. We shared everything imaginable, from the insignificant to the indispensable.

Forging a distinct identity was my first desire, and it never really diminished. As a result, my life's work is helping businesses and individuals discover, build, and amplify their unique "It" factor.

Discovering Your Desire

Before you start moonlighting as a drummer, launching your own catering business, or trying to stand apart from your twin, you must identify your desire. Your desire has to be burning; it can't be lukewarm. It should be unstoppable.

To start this process, consider what gives you passion and purpose. Ask yourself: If money were not an issue, how would I spend the rest of my life? Create a vision board with pictures, words, and quotes that allow you to hone in on your desire.

You needn't pick just one desire, either. While our focus is often on career success and wealth, make sure to also include personal desires, like running the New York City marathon. It's essential to nurture both our professional and personal lives.

Once you've determined your desires, make sure they're crystal clear. Running more often isn't specific enough, but completing the New York

City Marathon is. I believe in the importance of clarity so deeply that it's my company's philosophy: Make Yourself Perfectly Clear™.

Transforming Your Desire into Action

Identifying your desire is just the first step. You also need to take action to make it happen. Wealth, health, love, and anything else you desire will not simply appear in your life without effort. You need to put in the work. This means taking action, like changing your career or lifestyle.

When I say action, I mean intentional action. Throwing spaghetti on the wall doesn't turn desire into success. Instead, establish SMART goals. SMART stands for Specific, Measurable, Achievable, Realistic, and anchored within a Time Frame. Once you've listed five to eight goals (plus deadlines), determine the specific steps required to reach them.

Next, create a "Must Do" list. This is not a typo: "To Do" is too passive, so I prefer to call it a "Must Do" list. Ask yourself: "What must I do today to support my purpose and goals?"

Clear goals and Must Do's are critical to transforming desire into reality. When I started Co-Communications in the late 1990s in a spare bedroom, I aimed to create a PR and marketing agency that truly valued collaboration with its clients. While many think "Co" is part of my last name, it is actually from the Latin derivative meaning "with." The "Co" in Co-Communications stands for collaboration, which is a principle that allows us to develop long-lasting client relationships and is at the core of our team's success.

As you meet your goals and begin to reach your desire, raising the bar is essential. For me, that happened in 2010, when my passion for marketing and branding businesses morphed into personal branding. At first, this next step in my career was an accident, not a result of conscious goal setting. I was contacted by an organization that supports the underemployed, unemployed, and career transitioners.

"Would you speak to the organization's audience?" the director asked me. I agreed without a specific topic in mind but quickly had an epiphany. This unexpected pro bono speaking engagement helped me come to a major realization: Personal brands shouldn't be exclusive to Fortune 500 leaders, celebrities, or powerful politicos. They can and should be tools for everyone, from my daughter in high school to my 75-year-old retired father. Helping people be and communicate their best selves was my new burning desire.

I paired that new desire with goals and a "Must Do" list. And within a few years, I was advising on personal branding for the Huffington Post and on the TEDx stage.

Be The Change to Make it Happen

The bottom line? You have to own your desire and transmutation. And so, I'll end with six tips for doing just that:

Be open to change: Life doesn't happen by chance; it happens by choice and change. So, keep the doors open to new opportunities. All too often, we shut doors too quickly.

Discipline your mind to think positively: Thoughts transmute into reality. When you choose better thoughts, your world will show up differently. Flip negatives into positives and adopt a problem-solving mindset.

Surround yourself with positive and successful people: Spend time with family, friends, and business colleagues who root for you. Alternatively, avoid negative people who sap your energy.

Feed your mind: Inspirational books and podcasts are a great way to maintain your motivation and drive. My shelves are filled with inspirational business books to build my brain muscle, like *Mindset: The New Psychology of Success* (Carol S. Dweck, Ph.D.) and *Thrive* (Arianna Huffington).

Make it a habit: You need to stop overthinking and just DO it! In your everyday life, maintain a constant drumbeat of activity.

Practice gratitude: Whenever we feel negativity rising within us, we can counter it with gratitude for all the good in our lives. Feel thankful for what you already have.

As you seek success, let desire be the engine that propels you forward—and let transmutation be the engine that makes it real. Identify what you want, determine how to make it happen, and then get to work.

STACEY ROSS COHEN

About Stacey Ross Cohen: In the world of branding, few experts possess the savvy and instinct of Stacey. An award-winning brand professional who earned her stripes on Madison Avenue and major television networks before launching her own agency, Stacey specializes in cultivating and amplifying brands.

Stacey is CEO of Co-Communications, a marketing agency headquartered in New York. She coaches businesses and individuals across a range of industries — from real estate to healthcare and education — and expertly positions their narratives in fiercely competitive markets.

A TEDx speaker, Stacey is a sought-after keynote at industry conferences and author in the realm of branding, PR, and marketing. She is a contributor at Huffington Post and Thrive Global and has been featured in *Forbes, Entrepreneur, Crain's* and a suite of other media outlets. She holds a B.S. from Syracuse University, MBA from Fordham University and a certificate in Media, Technology and Entertainment from NYU Stern School of Business.

Author's website: *www.StaceyRossCohen.com*

Book Series Website & Author's Bio: *www.The13StepsToRiches.com*

Teresa Cundiff

MY MIND IS CONSUMED!

I don't know about you, but many times, when I get my mind set on something, I can think of little else. And it has run the gamut of subject matters from children's heartbreaks to waiting for my husband's next Army transfer order, to waiting for casting news of shows or waiting for job-related news—you get it. No doubt the same has happened to you. I always say, "My mind is consumed!" I find this is a great description of what is happening inside my head. I can't think of anything else, be effective at anything I'm doing, or really be of much help to anyone because all my gray matter is busy spinning over whatever has a hold of it!

This dilemma is a curse of the highest order because even though there will be an endpoint, I don't know when that will land. It could be the next time the phone rings, the email dings, or my husband walks in the door and says his transfer orders finally came, and we know where we're going. I will say I did learn to manage that one early on. The Army will always leave you hanging till the last minute. I just know that we are moving SOMEWHERE in the summer of whatever year, and my expectations will be fully managed. My point is, I would expend so much brain energy thinking about situations where other people had the information I needed or wanted. Imagine what I could do spending that energy on things I wanted or needed?

What if, instead, I took all that energy, thought, and power I was giving to what was "consuming my mind" and focused it elsewhere? That would be transmutation! And it would be a better and more productive use of my time, talents, and brain power. Each situation will resolve itself regardless of how I strain in its direction. So, if I take all that energy and transmute it into my business, relationships, or education, it would be a much better use than just toiling over what I can do nothing to improve.

It bears pointing out that a determination would have to be made as to whether I could actually make a change over the situations consuming me. It could be that I can, and if so, I most certainly should, and transmutation would not be appropriate. But I think being aware of when it's time to channel your energy in the right direction is easier than it sounds. Plus, in my case, I think I find a certain amount of comfort sitting in my mind being consumed, but I don't know why. Sometimes, you just have to be a grown-up and push ahead!

In October 1990, my husband deployed with the 101st Airborne (Air Assault) from Ft. Campbell, KY, to Operation Desert Shield/Desert Storm. Now, there was a thing that could consume a person's mind! However, I couldn't just stay home curled up in bed the whole time while he was gone, even though there were many days when that was all I wanted to do. CNN was the only news source back then, so when I wasn't at work, that was the only channel on the TV. My sister and I moved in together because her husband was gone as well, and she was pregnant. It was good for us to live together to support each other! Mind you, we were still living in our hometown with all our friends and family around us.

Even with all that support in place, I was still so lonely without my husband. We had married in March 1989, and now he was off to an unknown place fulfilling his duty as an Army officer, and I was left behind. I wrote him a letter every day that the mail ran and sent him a box every Saturday! But, of course, he didn't get a letter every day. The mail going over there didn't work that way. Days would go by with no mail at all for him, and then he'd get six letters! I sent him a tiny Christmas tree and all kinds of other stuff that had to be left behind.

It is 100% safe to say that my mind was consumed with all things "My Husband" all the time while we were separated. I would look at the moon and think, "At least we can both see the same moon." We only talked by phone three times during the whole seven months he was gone. It's nothing like today, where the service members get to talk face-to-face with their family members. I'm so glad it's different today. The separation is so painful to endure.

I had to transmute all my pain and sadness at being separated from my husband into useful activity for my own sake—and HIS! He not only had a job, but he also had a mission. He needed—yes needed—to know that I was doing well, keeping it together, keeping the bills paid, and doing okay. I couldn't be falling apart in my letters to him when he was halfway around the world fighting a war! Being a military spouse is not for sissies. Yes, we are sad, lonely, and cry, but the soldiers are going through so much more than we could ever contemplate. Especially way back then. We knew nothing of the enemy!

All my emotion was used to make everything better for him in every way I knew how! I only missed one day of work, and that was the day the ground war kicked off on January 17, 1991. I was just too much of an emotional wreck to face everyone at work. So, I allowed myself to sit in my emotions that day. I couldn't do anything else, and that was okay. My sister was a senior in college, so I think she had to make her classes that morning, but then she came home. We just sat together, glued to the television, watching Wolfe Blitzer.

My husband returned home on March 31, 1991. It was Easter Sunday that year. My brother-in-law had returned home two weeks before. I went to church that morning expecting my sister to join me, but she never showed up. She had gone into labor! There were no cell phones, so I went home after church to find out she was at the hospital. So, on that incredible day, Brian returned home, and Grace Victoria was born!

The Ft. Campbell Army band played for every plane that landed, and all the crowds went wild to welcome their soldiers home. Putting my arms around my husband finally allowed my mind to stop being consumed! Finally, he was home safe and sound! No chemical weapons had been used, and he would receive a clean bill of health, and we would try for a family now! In fact, on December 23, 1991, John Ryan was born!

I don't know if you have ever experienced anything that has consumed your mind for that long. I promise you it was no walk in the park. The times I thought I would break, I would think to myself, "My mother-in-law did two years of deployment with only one year in between when my father-in-law went to Vietnam, and she had three small boys! I can do this in my hometown with my friends and family around me."

Whenever you feel a great charge of energy, thought, or power building up inside of you and it's consuming you, and it's not focused where you want it, transmute that energy into action toward something else that needs your attention or someone else whom you can help. If it's consuming your mind, and you can't affect any change over the situation, pour all of that into something productive! I think it could have been so easy for me to spiral out of control, but knowing that my husband needed me to keep it together, I "kept the home fires burning," as we say. You never know the effect you can have on others by how you focus your energy. What you do matters because someone is always watching, and you are always influencing someone.

TERESA CUNDIFF

About Teresa Cundiff: Teresa hosts an interview digital TV show called Teresa Talks on Legrity TV. On the show, she interviews authors who are published and unpublished—and that just means those authors haven't put their books on paper yet. The show provides a platform for authors to have a global reach with their message. Teresa Talks is produced by Wordy Nerds Media Inc., of which Cundiff is the CEO.

Cundiff is also a freelance proofreader with the tagline, "I know where the commas go!" Teresa makes her clients work shine with her knowledge of grammar, punctuation, and sentence structure.

Teresa is a four-time international Bestselling contributing author of 1 Habit for Entrepreneurial Success, 1 Habit to Thrive in a Post-COVID World, The Art of Connection: 365 Days of Networking Quotes and The Art of Connection: 365 Days of Inspirational Quotes. The latter two are both placed in the Library of Congress. She is a 10-time Bestselling contributing author to The 13 Steps to Riches Series.

Author's Website: *www.TeresaTalksTv.com*

Book Series Website & Author's Bio: *www.The13StepsToRiches.com*

Vera Thomas

TRANSMUTED FOR SUCCESS!

"Still waters run deep
Our meaning of intimacy can deceive
And keep us from what can be
Our reality of a life
Beyond measure
We can unlock the hidden treasures
Intimacy need not just be a physical thing
Intimacy is ours to claim
From within the confines of our mind
When we set aside a little time
To expand our definition
Of what intimacy really means
Transmutation
Can be the beginning
Of healing ourselves and our nation."
~ Vera Thomas

Napoleon Hill devoted an entire chapter to transmutation. The definition of transmutation is "the action of changing or the state of being changed into another form." Hill talks about that change from physical desires to what can be equated to a type of spiritual awakening to a genius performance toward a successful life.

Napoleon Hill says that physical desire is the most powerful of human desires. When driven by this desire, men develop a keenness of imagination, courage, willpower, persistence, and creative ability unknown to them at other times. Love and romance are emotions capable of driving men to heights of super achievement. Combined, these emotions may lift one to an altitude of genius.

The chapter further explains that it is not so much our physical intimacy; it is the emotions of the act that drives one to success. Let us admit the feelings and emotions derived from having a special connection with another is second to none. Success can occur when those emotions are transmuted or changed to a higher form of expression. The higher forms of expression will transform into a mindset that exudes enthusiasm, creativity, and a mindset for success.

Hill defines transmutation as "the switching of the mind from thoughts of physical expression to thoughts of some other nature." This statement makes me think about Paul from the Bible; it appears Paul had reached the point of transmutation. All his drive and nature were transformed into doing the work God had purposed him to do. In fact, Paul also said, "For who hath known the mind of the Lord, that he may instruct him? But we have the mind of Christ." 1 Corinthians 2:16, KJV.

Napoleon Hill was a man of faith. In my opinion, *Think and Grow Rich* is representative of "the mind of Christ." If we are to demonstrate transmutation, we must reflect on what it means to have the mind of Christ as it relates to success. I would suggest having the "mind of Christ" represents much of what Napoleon Hill considered the keys to success.

I am by no means suggesting only people who are believers can exude transmutation. I am, however, suggesting having the mind of Christ is consistent with what Hill identifies as transmutation.

Christ made Himself of no reputation. While here on earth, the Holy One did not set out to make a reputation for himself. He walked in his purpose and fulfilled his duty even unto death. He demonstrated transmutation through his actions.

He took upon Him the form of a servant. As we pursue our goals and dreams aiming for success, having the mindset that whatever we are destined to do is not about us. I would equate this to what Hill calls the "perpetuation of mankind," a form of transmutation and a spirit of service to mankind.

He was made in the likeness of men. "The Word became flesh and dwelt among us" (John 1:14). As it is written in the Word, "Truly, truly, I say to you, whoever believes in me will also do the works that I do; and greater works than these will he do..." (John 14:12). Hill referenced scientific research which disclosed two significant facts: "The men of greatest achievement are men with highly developed natures." In fact, Hill further states, "The emotion is an irresistible force... when driven by this emotion, men become gifted with a superpower for action transmutation that will lift one to the status of a genius."

He humbled Himself. His humility was an expression of love. Transmutation is demonstrated through unconditional love first for self "when we develop a keenness of imagination, courage, willpower, persistence, and creative ability unknown..." (Hill).

He was Obedient unto death. This is a kind of intimacy that is a perfect example of transmutation. To live our true purpose that leads to success, having an intimate relationship with our higher power is the truest form of transmutation. Obedience is better than sacrifice.

This is the opportunity to listen to whatever it is you believe. The universe is full of all answers. We may get those answers through visions, dreams, that still small voice, or directly through the book of your belief. In my case, it is the Bible. Obeyance is one way to connect with one's higher calling.

Single-minded focus. Transmutation is when our physical, emotional, and spiritual drives are focused on living out one's purpose. This is exactly what Hill referred to in my earlier comments in this chapter. As he said, "When drives are harnessed and redirected along other lines, this motivating force maintains all of its attributes of keenness of imagination, courage, etc."

Christ was laser-focused, as was Paul, on the business of kingdom-building while healing, serving, and encouraging the masses. We, likewise, will realize all possibilities through transmutation from the physical to the spiritual.

Peaceful. The LORD gives perfect peace to those whose faith is firm. The Bible talks about three realms of peace: 1. Psychological peace, the comfort within; 2. Relational peace and harmony among humanity; 3. Spiritual peace, which is between God and man. Hill says, "The desire cannot, and should not be submerged or eliminated. But it should be given an outlet through forms of expression which enrich the body, mind, and spirit of man."

Peace comes when we harness and develop transmutation through creativity, imagination, willpower, persistence, etc. Peace and harmony among humanity through transmutation replace the physical realm. The intimacy between us and our higher power is a form of transmutation that gives peace beyond understanding.

To compare transmutation with the mind of Christ, one might have thought there is no correlation. But, in actuality, there are one hundred scriptures on the topic of transmutation! Here are just a few.

Genesis 1:1 ESV In the beginning, God created the heavens and the earth. 2. Now the earth was formless and empty, darkness was over the surface of the deep, and the Spirit of God was hovering over the waters.

If you believe in the creation theory, there is no better explanation for transmutation than this. He took nothing to create everything we know as the universe, heaven, and earth! Transmutation in the highest form!

Genesis 1:27 ESV So God created man in his own image, in the image of God he created him; male and female he created them.

Transmutation! Consider that we are the image of God! Think about that! Since we are the image of God and God dwells within us, can you imagine what this world would be like if we did live, breathe, and walk with purpose, knowing we are the image of God?

2 Corinthians 5:17 Therefore, if anyone is in Christ, he is a new creation; the old has gone, the new has come!

A perfect demonstration of transmutation. I believe this scripture is saying when we have the mind of Christ, all those negative behaviors and attitudes toward ourselves and others are transformed. Napoleon Hill's description of what happens with transmutation is much like what can be experienced when we are in Christ.

Creativity, imagination, and all the other attributes of transmutation represent being in Christ. Where there was a focus on anger, hate, bitterness, unforgiveness, and failure, all those things are changed to love, forgiveness, and the good success both Hill and the Bible speak about.

In conclusion, *Think and Grow Rich* is truly a roadmap that touches on all aspects of one's life. It is clear Napoleon Hill was a man of genius and a man of faith. I believe when a primary focus is one from a physical perspective, it limits possibilities and can stifle growth and transformation.

Transmutation is worth serious consideration for a heightened awareness of genius possibilities. Transmutation further supports that we are spiritual beings and that emotions can reach higher heights and deeper dimensions when we allow ourselves to harness our physical desires into aspects that lead to greater success and a deeper understanding of who we are and whose we are.

VERA THOMAS

About Vera Thomas: Vera Thomas lives in the state of Georgia. She is to date a 4x Bestselling Author, podcast host, certified transformation coach and family mediator, Classroom Management Advocate/trainer/speaker/poet. She works with parents, children, schools, organizations and churches.

Vera's life story directed her towards work with organizations that provided hope and empowerment to people like her to better themselves. It is her goal to help others overcome a circumstance that diminishes and help them to surge ahead with their dreams. Vera graduated "Cum Laude" with a Bachelor in psychology from Walsh University in Canton, OH.

Vera's work as a facilitator for more than three decades and includes developing training programs for youth and adults. Hear her story and think about your own. Vera is available for companies who want to transform their teams or individuals who want to transform their lives.

Author's Website: *www.linktr.ee/VeraThomaIinstillingGreatness*

Book Series Website & Author's Bio: *www.The13StepsToRiches.com*

Yuri Choi

TRANSMUTATION

Take a moment right now, as you are reading this, and put your hands on your belly or heart for a moment. Close your eyes and take a few deep inhales and exhales. Can you become aware of this powerful energy moving within you as you do this? This is the energy that keeps you moving, breathing, and living.

It's the energetic force that keeps your lungs breathing, your heart pumping, your stomach digesting, your blood flowing. This is your life force energy, your prana.

This energy is the most powerful force that runs through you, me, and all living organisms, individually and collectively. This energy can create, destroy, build, survive, thrive, build, expand, or contract, individually and collectively. Everyone has this energy running through them every day. How we channel and direct this energy each moment can change the environment and the reality we live in.

The question is, how consciously and intentionally are we directing this energy toward expansion and creation? How often are we letting this energy move towards fear-based actions and destruction, mostly because we are unaware that we are doing this or uninformed of how to powerfully transmute this energy into productive energy?

The first step is to become aware of your energy state and whether you are operating in a limited or creative energetic state.

How do you know what type of energy you are even operating in right now? Before you get to powerfully and consciously move your energy from a limited or creative state, one has to understand how to become aware of which energetics one is already operating in.

How do I know if I am in a limited energetic state?

Limited energy states are synonymous with fear-based, contractive, survival-driven energetic states. This is when one does things out of shame, guilt, fear, apathy, anger, and competition. As a result, one might feel constantly disempowered and tired. There are a few ways to see if you're currently operating in a limited mindset or energy state:

1. You feel that you are constantly competing.

2. You feel your worth and mood swinging up and down based on external factors.

3. You feel jealous or envious.

4. You feel scared or frozen.

5. You are feeling embarrassed.

6. You are feeling bored or uninterested.

7. You are feeling mad, frustrated, or stressed.

8. You are in the state of chasing after a feeling, things, or people.

9. Your energy often feels drained and low.

10. You are reacting to your stress or fear.

When operating in these states, the foundational core belief underneath it all is that there isn't enough for everyone. When there is a scarcity of resources, one must fight for survival to fight for these limited resources.

Therefore, one might feel that one must actively compete and combat with others rather than collaborate and help one another. One might find that putting others down to win this competition is necessary, rather than realizing that everyone can win, and others winning can also add to your success. One might feel uneasy or worried that their resources can be taken away if not guarded. One might feel embarrassed by or shameful of the belief that their resources are "less than" what others have, creating feelings of unnecessary insecurity.

One could even feel apathetic about life and people because they not aware that there could be infinite possibilities and adventures that life abundantly offers. Therefore, this person might often feel stressed and have to constantly chase the next shiny object or big milestone to feel enough or feel secure.

When one is in these energetic states, that core belief is that life is about survival and fear.

On the other hand, how do you know if you are in a creative mindset or set of energy states?

A creative mindset can be synonymous with abundant, limitless, love-based, and possibility-oriented energy states.

When you are in an abundant, creative mindset, these are some symptoms:

1. You feel that everyone can win and are genuinely excited when others win.

2. You are aware that there are limitless possibilities.

3. You feel peace, joy, and love often.

4. You are enthusiastic or optimistic about life and people.

5. You operate with flow and ease because you know that everything is happening for you.

6. You are grateful for what is given and excited about what's to come.

7. You feel worthy of all the blessings that have come your way already, as well as the ones that are about to come toward you.

8. You are giving, collaborative, and trusting others.

9. You can source boundless energy from your joy and inner peace.

10. You are responding from your heart and moving intentionally towards a vision you want to create for yourself and the world.

When operating in these abundant, creative states, the core belief is that we live in a world of infinite possibilities and the flow of eternal cosmic creativity. In these states, you are reminded that you are a creator—you are powerful and infinitely able. In these energetic states, you are fully activated as the powerful creator you are meant to be.

So, it's clear which state we want to mainly operate in. Now, you can identify if you are in a limited and fear-based energy state or a creative and abundant energy state. So then, how do you transmute limited energy states into powerful creative states?

Before I explain this, there is a Universal Law that you must know called the Law of Polarity. It states that everything has an equal and opposite energy. It's also applicable here. Every energy state can have an equal force of energy that can be moved in the other direction when intentionally channeled. This means every fear-based or limited energy state has an equal and opposite counterpart.

As a performance and fulfillment coach, I often go deeply into this type of transmutation of energy state with my high-achieving clients who want to create more flow, harmony, productivity, and focus in their lives.

By helping my clients understand how to become aware and direct their "negative" energy in powerful ways towards creation and expansion, they can create momentum by avoiding unnecessary conflicts and bottlenecks in their lives and businesses, allowing them to create more freely and more productively.

While I cannot cover all the ways this transmutation of energy can happen, I will share how you can transmute the energy of anger into optimism.

Anger is an energetic state that can activate massive action. Anger is also an energetic state that protects and honors boundaries and what's most important to that person, whether it be values, things, or people. However, when anger is not transmuted into creative, productive energy, it can turn violent and aggressive, leading to destruction rather than creation and expansion.

Imagine you have a dog you love dearly, and you were walking it down the street one day. Out of nowhere, this unleashed neighbor's aggressive dog ran after you, as if to attack. This really angered you and frightened you for a moment. What would you do, and how would you react or respond?

One thing you might do, out of anger, is try to attack the owner or the dog (violence) in reaction to your anger.

Another possibility is that you could become an energy alchemist and transmute that anger into love-based and expansive energy. Imagine that instead of getting angry and aggressive at the other dog and the owner, you peacefully talked to the dog owner about how this could have affected you and the other person negatively and how you both can protect yourselves from creating these situations in the future.

What if, instead of getting into a fight about it, you two collaborated to take massive actions about petitioning the city to create stricter leash laws and regulations to create a better environment for all pet owners?

Both reactions are massive actions and a response to the anger that one feels. The main difference is that one led to destruction and violence, and the other led to more order in the city? Which possibility would you rather choose? Which would be more productive and aligned with the energy of love?

By acknowledging the energy of anger and responding to it in a conscious, powerful, optimistic way, our anger can be transmuted into creating more order and peace in our worlds rather than aggression.

And truly, the more people can transmute fear-based energy to love-based energy, we all become alchemists and agents that turn this world into a better, more expansive, and loving place.

What could happen if you constantly chose to become the transmuter of energy into love-base and creative energy? How will you be transmuting the energies around you to be a part of the expansion of the world today?

YURI CHOI

About Yuri Choi: Yuri is the Founder of Yuri Choi Coaching. Choi is a performance coach for entrepreneurs and high achievers. She helps them create and stay in a powerful, abundant, unstoppable mindset to achieve their goals by helping them gain clarity and understanding, leverage their emotional states, and create empowering habits and language patterns.

She is a speaker, writer, creator, connector, YouTuber, and the author of Creating Your Own Happiness. Choi is passionate about spreading the messages about meditation, power of intention, and creating a powerful mindset to live a fulfilling life. She is also a Habitude Warrior Conference Speaker and emcee, and she is also a designated guest coach for Psych2Go, the largest online mental health magazine and YouTube Channel. Her mission in the world is to inspire people to live leading with L.O.V.E. (which stands for: laughter, oneness, vulnerability, and ease) and to ignite people's souls to live in a world of infinite creative possibilities and abundance.

Author's Website: *www.YuriChoiCoaching.com*

Book Series Website & Author's Bio: *www.The13StepsToRiches.com*

GRAB YOUR COPY OF AN OFFICIAL PUBLICATION
WITH THE ORIGINAL UNEDITED TEXT FROM 1937
BY THE NAPOLEON HILL FOUNDATION!

THE NAPOLEON HILL FOUNDATION
WWW.NAPHILL.ORG

Habitude Warrior Mastermind

Join a team of
AWESOME
Entrepreneurs, Coaches, Business Owners, and Leaders to support you in your journey of success!

Be one of my personal guests for a session!
www.MastermindGuestPass.com

www.ingramcontent.com/pod-product-compliance
Lightning Source LLC
Chambersburg PA
CBHW051300120626

46547CB00015B/2021

*978 1 9 6 4 3 3 0 1 2 9 *